Also by Dale Turner:

Different Seasons: Twelve Months of Wisdom & Inspiration

Grateful Living

GRATEFUL LIVING

Dale Turner

High Tide Press ‡ 1998

A HIGH TIDE BOOK
Published by High Tide Press Inc.
1910 Ridge Road, Homewood, Illinois 60430

Library of Congress Catalog Card Number: 98-070863
Turner, Rev. Dale E. Grateful Living / by Dale Turner – 1st ed.

ISBN 0-9653744-8-3

Printed in the United States of America
03 02 01 00 99 98   6 5 4 3 2 1

Book design by Alex Lubertozzi

First Edition

Printed on acid-free paper. ∞

To my wife, Leone

My children, Greg & Kathy,
Chuck & Linda, Bob, Drew & Pat

My grandchildren, Aaron & Robin,
Matthew, Heather, Brittany, Evan,
Carl, Marshall, and Russell

Be kind. Everyone you meet
is carrying a heavy burden.

—Ian MacLaren

CONTENTS

[*ix*]

Preface

IN WRITING HIS autobiography, G.K. Chesterton wanted to find one sentence that described what life was all about. In that one sentence he said, "The critical thing is whether we take life for granted or whether we take it with gratitude." Living with an attitude of gratitude is helpful to ourselves and to those who live around us. It is with gratitude for your readership that I submit these columns. I hope there will be something interesting or useful in them for you.

When I published my first collection of *Seattle Times* columns in book form, *Different Seasons*, I had hoped to reach a few people with some insights that might be helpful to them in their everyday lives. I was unprepared for the overwhelming response, not only from people in Washington, but from around the country. It is a humbling experience to know that people I've never met before are picking up my book and reading with care the words I've written. It is also a bit frightening when I think of the responsibility that comes with it.

So I am grateful to be allowed a forum in which to share my thoughts and observations. And I am grateful to God for allowing me to continue doing what it is I love—reaching out to people and, hopefully, making a difference for the better in their lives.

Grateful living is a philosophy that affirms, on a daily basis, how much we have to be thankful for. Indeed, God does not give us all things so that we may enjoy life, but gives us life that we may enjoy all things. As the English poet Thomas Gray put it:

> *Sweet is the breath of vernal shower,*
> *The bee's collected treasures sweet,*
> *Sweet music's melting fall, but sweeter yet*
> *The still small voice of gratitude.*

If our minds are inhabited by a grateful philosophy, then our bodies can't help but follow suit. For when we think with gratitude, we act with gratitude.

Dale E. Turner
Seattle, Washington
May 1998

Grateful Living

GIVING

The widow's mite.
christ gave.

Giving Thanks

"GRATITUDE," SAID MARTIN Luther, "is the basic Christian attitude." Perhaps Thanksgiving is the most basic holiday of all, for without an attitude of gratefulness, Christmas, Hanukkah, Easter, and other high and holy days would never be fully appreciated or understood.

Gratitude can be expressed in a variety of ways. Sometimes it takes the form of grace before a meal. Within the home, the blessing is usually meaningful to all, but grace before the meal at a public banquet can sometimes be an awkward situation, because so many varieties of thinking are represented at the tables. Occasionally a prayer at a public function is phrased in such a way as to be acceptable to all, and in some situations, the prayer is so unique or different that it proves to be a stimulator of discussion during the meal that follows.

Such a situation occurred years ago at a banquet where I was the speaker. The chairman of the meeting created a model for brevity when he prayed simply, "Eternal God, Thanks. Amen." That was it. No more. He

[5]

left it up to us to spell out what it was for which we were thankful. I was as startled as everyone else. Predictably, the prayer did create some discussion and not a few smiles from those seated at the tables. Following the meeting, one of the chairman's friends, with a twinkle in his eye, asked, "How did you ever find the time to prepare?" In one word the chairman had captured the essence of gratitude—thoughtfulness.

During the meal I found myself remembering a rhyme I had learned as a child:

> *Thanks is just a little word*
> *No bigger than a minute*
> *But there's a world of meaning*
> *and appreciation in it.*

Perhaps because the word *thanks* is so small is why it is so often overlooked or considered unimportant by so many. It is amazing how otherwise intelligent people often overlook this little amenity, forgetting that it is as important to acknowledge a favor as it is to bestow one.

Such neglect is not new. In the book of Luke, Chapter 17, verses 12-17, we read of ten lepers who were cleansed by Jesus, but only one returned to say thanks. The ingratitude of the nine was a worse leprosy than the disease itself.

Conscientious parents begin early in training their children to express thankfulness for favors bestowed. Robert Louis Stevenson was reared in a home where expressions of gratitude were ingrained in every day's living. It is not surprising that in one of his stories he tells of a wayfarer in France who slept so peacefully one summer night in a meadow under a canopy of stars that in the morning, out of sheer gratitude, he whimsically emptied the coins in his purse on the ground and left them there in payment for the unstinted hospitality which he had received. True religion is suggested by the episode. All people at their best feel they must show gratitude to someone for favors received.

Happy are we if we know that all of our blessings are traceable to God's goodness. Every furrow in the Book of Psalms is sown with seeds of thanksgiving. How wise to memorize significant passages and make them our own:

> It is a good thing to give thanks unto the Lord and to sing praises unto thy name most high.
>
> O that we would praise the Lord for His goodness and for His wonderful works to the children of men.
>
> Bless the Lord, O my soul, and all that is within me, bless His holy name. Bless the Lord, O my soul, and forget not all his benefit.

With all the benefits for which we have reason to rejoice, we are aware, too, of hungry and homeless people near at hand and throughout the world.

The sense of our abundance and good fortune must beget an equal sense of compassion, charity, and generosity, or we are in peril of moral deterioration.

Our earnest prayers rise daily, imploring God to guide our leaders toward finding a path to peace. We pray, too, that we would do anything to share our plates of food with the hungry everywhere. But as we pray, relief agencies are hard at work trying to stretch their minimal supplies.

Prayer is a two-way street. We can hear God answer that there are things that we can do. There are ways to share. There is need for staple food and money in the relief centers of our own city. We need only to respond. The best way to make glad the heart of the heavenly Father is to do something for one of his other children.

Jamie Alford, an American poet expresses a dimension of gratitude that is worthy of emulation:

> *I do not thank Thee, Lord,*
> *That I have bread to eat while others starve:*
> *Nor yet for work to do*
> *While empty hands solicit heaven:*
> *Nor for a body strong*
> *While other bodies flatten beds of pain.*
> *No, for these I do not give thanks!*
> *But I am grateful, Lord,*
> *Because my meager loaf I may divide:*
> *For that my busy hands*
> *May move to meet another's need;*
> *Because my doubled strength*
> *I may expend to steady one who faints.*
> *Yes, for all these I do give thanks!*
> *For heart to share, desire to bear*
> *And will to lift.*
> *Flamed into one deathless love*
> *Thanks be to God for this! Unspeakable! His Gift!*

∼

All Are Touched

HERE IS AN interesting incident in the life of the disciple Peter that is recorded in the fifth chapter of the Book of Acts. The fame of Peter had spread far and wide. When people heard that he was passing through Jerusalem, they brought their sick and infirm and placed them on beds and cots along the roadside, with the hope that Peter's shadow might fall upon the ill and they would be healed.

In our scientific age, this would certainly strike many as superstition of the highest order. It would be magic. To expect healing in a shadow seems unthinkable. Yet there is a universal truth in this narrative that deserves to be pondered.

Each of us has a shadow of influence that follows wherever we go. For good or ill, it falls on others. Silently, it reaches where we are not aware, and often touches those we had not intended. Emerson states it well in his poem, "Each and All":

> *Not knowest thou what argument*
> *Thy life to thy neighbor's creed has lent.*

All are needed by each one;
Nothing is fair or good alone.

The shadow of our mother's influence falls upon us even before we are born, and the environment of our early home is with us forever—"A leaf never falls far from the trunk."

Relationships beyond the home soon begin to shape our lives, and it is understandable why conscientious parents want to know their children's companions. Peer pressure induces actions for good or ill, and copybooks are full of maxims that warn of the harmful effects of unfortunate associations.

Happily, there are those who spread joy and health wherever they go. Robert Browning, in one of his classics, pictures the transforming effect of a little girl whose name was Pippa. She makes her way through a street where despair, disappointment, and defeat are the dominant notes.

When Pippa passes, all is different. Every home on the street feels the effect of her song and radiant personality. She sings because there is a joyous song in her heart. Passing through, she lifts drooping spirits and cheers the very atmosphere of that drab neighborhood.

It was said of George Washington that he moved among his soldiers like a magnet, silently, nobly drawing from his men all their dormant potential for good.

Sometimes, even an inanimate object—a portrait or work of art—will cast a helpful shadow. In a gallery in Europe there is a statue of Apollo, a Greek god. He is muscular, tall and straight. Guides who take tourists

through that gallery have pointed out that, quite uncon-
sciously, tourists who are tired, weary and slumped will
straighten up in the presence of the marvelous statue.

It is well known that in sports we often fall or rise to
the level of our competition. Some time ago, I played in
a golf foursome with three friends who are among
Seattle's better golfers. I was the hacker. I should have
been carrying their bags, for the only way I will ever play
in the 90s is to live that long!

Yet, somehow, in the company of those three excellent golfers, I was able to play a better round than usual.
My friends were helpful to me, not in setting out to
instruct me, but in the very manner of their play.

Conscientious people accept responsibility for what
their lives may mean in influencing others, but they
shun the image of model or mentor. They know their
own inadequacies and, to them, posing or pretending
superiority is a most obnoxious fault.

However, when we consider the matter of influence
more carefully, we see that it is not a thing of choice or
conscious design, but an inevitable and inherent relation from which no one escapes.

As the lives of those around her were changed by
Browning's Pippa, so the life of a whole community is
sometimes transformed for good in its ideals and aims
by people who have never thought of themselves in
terms of trying to be an influence or deserving to be an
example.

But in loyalty to their own highest ideals, they walk
steadily and constantly toward the light of justice, honor,
and truth, and the shadow of good influence falls

behind them.

They attract rather than compel others toward goodness, luring them by the appeal of their own integrity and love.

Be noble, and the nobleness that lies in
Others, sleeping but never dead
Shall rise in majesty to meet thine own
Then shalt thou see it gleam in many eyes
Then shall pure light around thy path be spread
And thou shalt nevermore be sad or lone.

∾

Kinds of authority, or influence, that given by the "System" and that earned by the leader

A Priceless Gift

 URING THE TIMES of the year when we give gifts to those we love and to those we know to be in need, we discover anew the job that gifts can bring—both in the giving and in the receiving. We also rediscover how costly gifts can be—moreso with every passing year.

We often wish we had more money so we could buy bigger and better gifts and give more to those in need. But, for many people, money is in short supply. I heard one man remark the other day that there were still many days until Christmas, and already his disposable income had been disposed of.

Yet, there is good news for those who have limited resources with which to buy for others. There are intangible gifts that can supplement the tangible gifts we can afford and that also may be given not only now, but throughout the year—a type of promissory note.

I suggest just two: the gift of praise and the gift of physical presence. The two seem so simple and commonplace, yet they are too often neglected or overlooked.

*praise your wife!
and your kids!*

*famous author
grateful for letter
from Jr. high class*

Two groups of people we often neglect to affirm or praise are those within the family circle, and those leaders or folks on top who appear to already have it made and who wouldn't seem to be in need of additional strokes.

Ralph Waldo Emerson was such a noted personality. No one would have believed he had need of further affirmation from family and friends. Yet he once wrote: "I need the daily praise and encouragement that comes from those close to me, and others, to help me live at my best. I cannot do it on my own."

Bill Russell, former Boston Celtic great and one-time coach of the Seattle Super Sonics, tells of his college days when he was a member of the San Francisco Dons, NCAA championship basketball team of 1955-56. Russell was the star of the team. Without him, the team was no more than average.

Yet, the coach neglected to praise Russell. This saddened and hurt him and, finally, at the end of the season, he told the coach of his disappointment.

The coach said that he thought that other players were the ones who needed praise, for Russell's name was constantly in the newspaper headlines and his fans were numbered in the thousands. "Yes, I know, and I appreciate that," responded Russell, "but it was from you, my coach and my friend, that I most needed to hear words of praise."

Wilt Chamberlain, seven-feet, one-inch tall, and one of Russell's chief competitors throughout their basketball careers, said, "Nobody roots for Goliath." That's too bad. Goliath, the boss, the powerful, the rich, the political leaders all need praise and affirmation for work well done, as much as do "little guys."

It is lonely at the top, and the realization that people notice and care what kind of person you are, and what you are doing can be powerful motivation. The influence some Goliaths have is enormous, and if we take the time to speak or write to them a word of gratitude, the ripple may touch many.

One of the great injustices we perpetrate upon ourselves, and others, is to have a good impulse and then neglect or refuse to act on it.

> *A kindly word was in my mind*
> *I never set it free.*
> *It died from lack of exercise*
> *And made its tomb in me.*

I was reminded of the importance of physical presence by reading the conversation that Leigh Mitchell Hodges, the noted writer, had with a prosperous businessman the day before Christmas.

"Would you like to know," asked the businessman, "what I am giving my boy for Christmas?" Realizing that this father could give a costly gift, Hodges replied that he would like to know. The man then handed a paper to Hodges, on which was written:

"To my dear son: I give you one hour each week day, and two hours on Sundays, to be yours, to be used as you want them, without interference of any kind whatsoever. Love, Your Father."

Hodges smiled in surprise. He wondered what the

boy would think and feel on Christmas morning. He wondered if he would realize the value of the gift. "Tell me," said Hodges, "how did you hit upon the idea of giving such an unusual present?"

The man answered, "The other day a young fellow whom I had not seen since he was a lad came to my office to 'make a touch.' His face and bearing carried the telltale marks of idleness and dissipation. 'Robert,' I exclaimed in amazement, 'I'm surprised to see you like this! And you with such a fine father!'

"The boy answered, 'Well, I have often heard that my dad was a fine man. All his friends have told me so. I never knew him. He was so occupied with his business and his clubs that I only saw him occasionally at mealtimes. I never really knew him.'

"That made me think—and think furiously—and believe me, from now on, I'm going to see to it that my son has a chance to know me, be it for good or bad. I know now that the greatest gift a man can give—a gift that every father owes his child—is a little time—his physical presence."

Simple gifts—but symbols of love and caring—life's greatest virtues.

∾

Forgiveness

WO OF THE most important lessons in life are learning how to be forgiven and learning how to be forgiving.

The best way to keep the home fires burning is with the chips from our own shoulders. How many homes could be radically transformed if those who lived in them were more forgiving? God has forgiven all of us so much that surely we can forgive members of our own family who have sinned against us so little.

Forgiveness does not leave the hatchet handle sticking out of the ground. Forgiveness is complete—buried forever.

We often have opportunities to forgive others for little infractions. The infractions may be small, but the manner of forgiving or not forgiving is not a small thing. For instance, how do we respond when someone has dialed the phone incorrectly and reached us by mistake?

I have had people respond to me in a gruff and angry manner when I have dialed incorrectly, and have been left feeling stupid for having made such an error. But there are others who have been kindly and understanding. One said to me, "It's okay. It's no big deal. Hope you reach the party you want to reach."

The manner of our response is a picture window through which another may look to discover a great deal about our personality. Some have been so kind to me when I made a mistake and dialed incorrectly that I have wished I could have visited with them and gotten to know them better.

One couple I know dialed a friend to sing happy birthday to him. When finished, they discovered that they had dialed the wrong number. The listener who had heard them (and their apology) said, "Oh, that's okay. You needed the practice, anyhow."

Sometimes we have opportunities to forgive serious transgressions. Many years ago on a Sunday when new people were received into membership in our church, I forgot to read the name of one man who was to join. As the others came forward to be welcomed into membership, the man whose name was not read remained in his seat.

The very sad fact of my omission was that this particular person had pondered membership for a long time, and his decision to join was a most important commitment. He had invited relatives and friends from near and far to be with him to share in his high hour. There were fourteen or fifteen in that group. But I forgot to read his name!

I became aware of my mistake at the close of the service when the head usher said to me, "Dale, a man left here this morning, livid with rage. He said he was to have joined the church and was left out. A lot of the people with him didn't seem too happy, either."

I checked my list and saw my mistake. Oh man, how should I handle this? I wished I could disappear, but no, I'd have to face it. So after lunch, I went to the home of the one I had omitted. I walked back and forth in front for many minutes before I had the courage to knock.

I was met at the door by the "non-member" and I blurted out, "I blew it today and I've come to say I'm very, very sorry."

A smile broke across his face and he said, "Thanks for coming here today. It's not all your fault. I should have had the good sense to get out of my seat and come forward without having my name read, so it was partly my fault, too. Come in and meet my family and some friends who are here. Why don't you stay and eat with us?"

I felt like a prodigal son welcomed back from a far county and invited to share in a banquet, my sins forgiven. I had already eaten, but I ate again. I needed the supporting community of love as never before. When I was to leave his home, my friend asked, "When are new members to be received next? I'll be there." And he was.

What a burden that beautiful man lifted from my shoulders that day. He was even magnanimous in accepting some of the blame, and set me free to relate to him with an at-oneness, for there was no resentment or animosity in his life. He is now deceased, but I think of him and his kindness time and time again.

The great souls of history have always been generous in forgiveness. Who can think of Lincoln without recalling his words: "with malice toward none, with charity for all."

Stephen, the first Christian martyr, was killed by stoning, and while dying, he said, "Lay not this sin to their charge."

Jesus was the victim of indescribable cruelty and injustice, yet in those agonizing moments on the cross, Jesus prayed, "Father, forgive them, for they know not what they do."

It is no mystery why the words of Isaac Newton move us all:

> *When I survey the wondrous cross*
> *On which the prince of glory died,*
> *My richest gain I count but loss*
> *And pour contempt on all my pride.*
> *Were the whole realm of nature mine*
> *That were a present far too small.*
> *Love so amazing, so divine,*
> *Demands my life, my soul, my all.*

Share the Wealth

ONEY BEARS THE brunt of many jokes and humorous comments, such as: A butterfly is the second most beautiful thing with wings, the first is money; Money no longer talks, it merely snickers, and; An income is what you cannot live without or within.

Despite the jests that surround things financial, nothing deserves to be taken more seriously than money. Learning to use money lovingly, wisely, and unselfishly is one of the most neglected areas of teaching in home and school.

Money is not merely something we carry in our pockets. It is an extension of our personalities. It is also an indicator of where our interests really lie and the use we make of it determines the ends our lives will serve.

One of our deepest needs is an intelligent appreciation of money's worth. Money is not filthy lucre, as some would contend. It is one of life's greatest goods. Its possession makes possible food, clothing, and shelter. It opens the door for travel, recreation, education, and healthcare. It enables us to give to others to meet our spiritual needs and sense of self-worth.

George Bernard Shaw said, "I do not recall running into many people in my life for whom money was not a problem of some kind. For the majority, of course, the difficulty is not having enough of it." From his experience, he continued, "It was not the love of money, but the lack of money that was the root of all evil."

There is confirmation of Shaw's observation. Ninety percent of all crime is committed for money. Money, more than any other thing, is at the bottom of marital troubles. Often, the most worthy political candidates are not elected because they did not have adequate resources to fully publicize their aims and aspirations, and gain name familiarity.

It seems as though most people want more money than they have. We can all appreciate the caption on the cartoon of a man working on the family bills who says, "We seem to be in the middle-income, upper-outgo group."

Despite any privations we may feel, we are still among the top one percent of privileged people in the world. Most of us have beds, clothes, food, family, and friends to love us, cars to drive, work to do, available medical care, and countless libraries and churches where we can find stimulus for mental and spiritual growth.

Every year, religious institutions, the United Way, political parties, and a host of other worthy enterprises set before us opportunities to express gratitude for our privilege, and concern and compassion for needy people and worthy causes. The organizations and institutions seeking our help are not beggars on the world's doorstep, but brokers encouraging us to share our resources—few or many—in constructive ways.

There are those who have great respect for the churches and for United Way, but give little support. They are willing to give credit, but reluctant to give cash—at least, to give in proportion to their ability to give. It is a source of concern for those who lend in financial efforts that many do not accept their proportionate share. It is a concern because it limits the good that can be done, and denies the giver the joy of whole-hearted participation. If we do not have charity in our hearts, we have the worst kind of heart trouble.

We all have our favorite special causes, but we should also not forget United Way and the religious institutions that touch so much of life in many crucial areas of need. As contributors, we can do the work of compassion and healing where our own footsteps can never tread. Those who determine where and how the monies will be distributed in our churches, United Way, and other benevolent services are the wisest of stewards. They scrupulously guard against unwise allocations and expenditures. To use the language of Wall Street, they are able to provide us with a "good investment spread."

I keep remembering the old baseball story that is relevant to the present. Charlie Grimm was at one time manager of the Chicago Cubs. The Cubs were having a disastrous year and were in a long losing streak. But one day in the midst of that miserable slump, one of Grimm's scouts phoned excitedly from the hinterlands. "Charlie, Charlie," he shouted with joy, "I've just seen the greatest pitcher in the country. He pitched a perfect no-hit, no-run game! Twenty-seven strikeouts! No one even hit a foul ball off him until there were two out in the ninth. I've got him here now. What shall I do?"

"Sign the guy that got the foul," said Grimm. "Our team needs hitters!" That is what our community needs today, hitters—financial hitters—if we are to measure up to the responsibilities and opportunities that are ours. Privilege humbly possessed and unselfishly shared is one of a person's noblest deeds.

The Perfect Gift

T EVERY GIFT-GIVING occasion, we ponder what to buy for those we love that will meet their needs or desires and be within our budget. Liston Pope, a former dean of Yale Divinity School, suggested two criteria in gift giving.

"The perfect gift," said Pope, "should reflect the individuality of the giver and, at the same time, correspond to the wishes and needs of the recipient."

As difficult as finding this kind of gift may be, in the following rhyme, Edgar Guest calls our attention to another suggestion:

> *If I were Santa this year*
> *I'd change his methods for the day*
> *I'd give to all the children dear*
> *But some things I would take away.*

This idea tickles the imagination. What would you take away if you were Santa for a day? Mr. Guest suggests many aggravations from which he would be happy to be separated—heartaches, pain, care, fears, doubts, bitter griefs. To be sure, most of us could add to his list. We'd be happy to have a little less rain, less traffic, and a little less that needs to be done each day.

Here's what I'd add:

I wish I were beside a lake,
Or sitting in a boat,
With all the things I've got to write,
Wrote.

But would we really want to live forever on a sun-swept plateau of painless comfort and fearless pleasure? Would we want all our doubts and fears removed for good, here and now?

Without sorrow, the palate is dulled so that we become unable to taste joy. We are like the man who dines so luxuriously each day that he becomes indifferent to food. After a period of starvation, however, he can taste the exquisite flavor of even a piece of dry bread.

The more we know about disabilities and experiences with people who have disabilities, the more we realize that our minds and spirits are either our greatest allies or our greatest hindrances in orienting ourselves in varying life situations. If there is no handicap in the mind, there is no real handicap.

Richard Bach, in his book *Illusions,* offers a thought worth remembering: "There is no such thing as a problem without a gift for you in its hand."

Francis Bacon said, "Whoever hath anything fixed in his person that doth induce contempt, hath also a perpetual spur in himself to rescue and deliver himself from scorn." Bacon spoke from experience, for his own suffering drove him to become one of England's greatest philosophers.

It is said that Byron's club foot made him fight to prove his superiority in literature and made him a swimmer expert enough to cross the Hellespont between Europe and Asia.

Helen Keller, although deaf, blind, and unable to speak, discovered the magic of transformation through which she lived such a rich and full life. "I thank God," she wrote, "for my handicaps, for through them, I have found myself, my work, and my God."

Franklin D. Roosevelt once told a close friend he thought his crippled condition was an asset. He explained that while others might be tempted to get up now and then to look out the window or stretch their legs, he was riveted to his desk and thus was able to concentrate on his work.

Things do turn out best for those who make the best of the way things turn out.

Phillips Brooks' early ambition was to be a teacher. Upon graduation from college, he launched his career in teaching. But he found he was a failure as a teacher. The students made him tired and cross. He was humiliated by his lack of control over them. So he quit teaching and went into seclusion, refusing to see even his close friends.

He was able to turn his negative experience into positive gain, however, and entered the Christian ministry, becoming one of America's greatest preachers and author of one of our favorite Christmas carols, "O Little

Town of Bethlehem."

The mountains were made when God's firm foot pressed out the valleys. In God's creative design, both have their own beauty. If we had no shadowy valleys, we would have no brilliant mountain tops.

If we are going to take away anything this year, let's be sure we take away the right things.

> He asked for strength that he might achieve;
> He was made weak that he might obey.
> He asked for health that he might do greater things,
> He was given infirmity that he might be better things.
> He asked for riches that he might be happy;
> He was given poverty that he might be wise.
> He asked for power that he might have the praise of men;
> He was given weakness that he might feel the need of God.
> He asked for all things that he might enjoy life;
> He was given life that he might enjoy all things.
> He received nothing he asked for—all that he hoped for,
> His prayer is answered—he is most blessed.

LIVING

Useful Ruts

 NEWS RELEASE TELLS of a bus driver in the Bronx who took the wheel of his bus and instead of driving his route, which he had done conscientiously for sixteen years, week in and week out, he drove all the way to Florida

When questioned about his unscheduled tour, he simply said he was fed up with the daily routine and just wanted to get away from it all. It is not difficult to relate to the mood that prompted that bus driver's excursion. There are occasions when most of us would like to chuck it all, break the bonds of habit, and get away from the routine that is so daily and so often overpowering.

A witty bishop was once asked why he kept a summer home which he seldom visited. "Do you not know," he replied, "that I must have someplace where though I never go to it, I can always imagine that I might be happier than where I am." It is a strange quirk of human nature that so often we wish to be elsewhere than where we actually are.

Vicki Baum, in the fine book *Grand Hotel*, describes this discontent. She writes:

The real thing is always going on somewhere else. When you are young you think it will come later. Later on you think it was earlier. When you are here, you think it is there. When you get there you find that life has doubled back and is quietly waiting here, here in the place you ran away from.

It is the same with life as it is with the butterfly collector and the swallowtail. As you see it flying away it is wonderful, but as soon as it is caught, the colors are gone and the wings bashed.

No matter how exciting or important a person's work may be, there is always much that is routine and even boring. Dr. Charles Eliot was president of Howard University from 1869 to 1909. One day he said, "My work offers me, I imagine, more variety than the work of most professional men. Yet at least nine-tenths of my work has now come to be routine. It brings me no more novelty or fresh interest than the work of a carpenter or blacksmith brings to him."

Whatever our home or work situation may be it is normal to have days when we are low in spirit. No life runs continuously on an even keel. The desire to escape from routine does not mean that we are lazy or are not conscientious. It means that we need the variation which is a law of life. A violin string that remains taut will snap. Those who hold on must learn to let go.

While some alternation of activity is wise and necessary in a well-ordered life, still it is wisdom to be aware of the values of routine.

We tend to think of ruts as bad peruse. That is not

necessarily so. Think of the great train, the Empire Builder. What a rut that train is in! Day after day it is stuck in its four-foot, eight-inch groove. Over and over again it travels the same path—Seattle to Spokane to Whitefish to Fargo to Minneapolis to Chicago and back again.

Years ago this family of cars added a dome car as part of its equipment. With this new asset it might have felt qualified to wander a bit where views would be more spectacular and the trip less routine. Fortunately, for everyone aboard, the Empire Builder did not veer from its appointed course. Until the end of its days the train will be in its same old rut. Precisely because it is satisfied to remain in its rut it will continue to he a great and useful train.

It is possible to energize the usual and to infuse into the daily that which is creative and exciting. One of life's chief joys is to take a little plot of land, barren, rocky, and unpromising, and till it so conscientiously and creatively that something beautiful will grow where only that which was drab and unattractive had been.

That is what Peter Milne did. His mission assignment placed him on the little island of Nguana in the New Hebrides. What an unpromising situation it was. But Peter Milne was committed to turning minuses into pluses.

He dedicated himself to his work so totally and did it in such an inspiring way that under his picture in the church he founded, the natives placed the words: "When he came there was no light. When he died there was no darkness.

Whoever we are and wherever we are and however routine life's situation may appear to be, there is something fine and good that God can do through us that apart from us will never get done. Ours is a sacred trust.

❧

Freedom

REEDOM IS PERHAPS the most cherished state of all being. But when it comes to defining or understanding it we cannot. The very nature of freedom defies a single definition, and understanding freedom becomes a lifelong study.

It is common to think of freedom as the right to do as we please without inhibitions, prohibitions, or restraints. Such a concept leads only to personal and public chaos. There can be no well-organized personal life or order in society without restraints. The free and easy, do-as-you-please attitude fails to reckon with the necessity of civil law, custom, moral standards, or anything that hinders the pleasure of the moment. Freedom is the right to be wrong, but not the right to do wrong.

There are those who will say, "This is a free country," implying, "I can do as I please." The statement is correct, but the conclusion is not. This is a free country, but we cannot do as we please. We cannot speed down the main street of any city at seventy miles an hour and we cannot help ourselves from the cash drawer of the bank

or the place of our employment. We soon find that freedom is limited. We are free only within the laws of
nature and of our society. A fish is not free to live on
land, and man is not free to live underwater or on the
surface of the moon without life-sustaining supports.

Freedom for unbridled, irresponsible action would
be a detriment to society. If what I might want to do
might harm another, am I free to do it? Am I free to
shout fire in a crowded building if there is no fire? My
freedom to shout is restrained by my surrender to a
higher law of restraint, my concern for people, and what
might happen to them if I misuse my liberty.

If inner restraint is not volunteered we must be
restrained from without. Prisons are filled with men and
women who did not or could not practice voluntary
restraint. Edmund Burke said, "There must be restraint
on human will and appetite somewhere. The less there
is from within, the more there must be from without. It
is contrary to the eternal constitution of things that men
of intemperate minds can be free."

The well-ordered personal life demands certain
restrictions. We cannot say "yes" to some good things in
life unless we are ready to say "no" to others. Those who
want a slim figure know they can have it only by saying
no to desserts.

Those who seek to be entirely independent, to be
free to do as they please and be their own masters, often
become slaves to the worst of masters, their own
appetites. When we surrender to our appetites, we soon
lose moral sense and energy, and become incapable of
discerning and practicing good. Habits too weak to be

felt become too strong to be broken. Surrendering to an inner anarchy of desire eventually gives birth to outer anarchy. In the moral life, we are governed by our desires. Obedience is not the mark of a slave. It is an important quality in a well integrated life. The great leaders of the world have not been their own masters, but have followed someone higher than themselves, and have thereby become greater. Obedience and self-surrender are gateways to power. Strength of character issues from obedience to the decree of conscience. If we are to have a commanding hold on life, we must be subject to a will higher than our own.

When we examine human greatness, we will always find that it consists of human spirits finding some cause or principle or person and giving self up to it. There is no greatness that is not self-surrender. Only one who has been mastered by something or someone worth being mastered by can ever be a whole and noble person.

We may wonder sometimes what religion does for us. It does not answer all of our questions or save us from trouble and grief. But it does free us from bondage to a lesser end. The glory and beauty of a worthy religion is that it sets us free from self-pride, apathy, and satisfaction with mediocrity. It rescues us from dogmatism, and keeps us conscious of our family and our need of God's grace.

When we surrender to God's will of divine love, self-fulfillment and public usefulness is found. This is what it means to be saved.

We are rescued from an unbridled, purposeless life

that is going nowhere to one that has eternal purpose and glows with meaning. God does not coerce into obedience or surrender, but draws us by his love.

Myth Comes Alive

 NE OF THE most captivating of mythological characters was Procrustes. He was the robber who was not content to merely rob and plunder. His eccentricity was to make each one of his victims lie down on an iron bed and be fitted to it. If they were too short, he had them stretched on the rack. If they were too long, he lopped off their extremities. He insisted that no one should be taller or shorter than he. Procrustes was his own standard of perfection.

The truth is that Procrustes is not a myth. He stalks the Earth today under the guise of social custom, conformity, regimentation, still insisting on uniformity, standardization, like-mindedness.

Replicas of the iron bed are in mass production. We put a premium on conformity. We often penalize originality, ingenuity, personal initiative, and distinctiveness. This is the age of the homogenized man and woman. The individual is giving way to the mass.

Motion pictures and television dictate our styles and sometimes our morals. Columnists and commentators provide us with premasticated ideas. Book clubs select our reading. We are encouraged to do our thinking by eye and ear, and our acting by imitation. We parrot the ideas of those about us. We live under a dictatorship of psychological pressure and social atmosphere.

The purpose of education is not to teach us what to think, but how to think—how to gather data, analyze, compare, make intelligent judgments that issue in wise actions. But, as Sarah H. Lawrence writes, this is not always what happens. "Education," she observes, "was once a teacher on one end of a log—a student on the other. Today we see a logjam with students astride their whirling floats heading toward the sawmill, where they will be ground into pulp and reappear mass-produced into millions of identical, wooden-headed molds."

The move toward sameness is encouraged by high-powered advertising, the great conditioner of customs and creator of appetites. Every strategy is used to keep products moving and to develop habits. Advertising agencies seem to ponder the advisability of making entertainment dull, so that commercials are exciting by contrast. In several instances, they have succeeded to excess. A good television mystery would be one where it would be difficult to detect the sponsor.

Fair people have no quarrel with advertising, per se. Advertisers make worthwhile TV and radio programs possible. They alert us to products and services that are available. Unfortunately, some advertising discourages personal initiative and distinctiveness. Their appeal is often to vanity or envy. Your neighbor has this, why can't you? Do you want to be different? No, of course not.

Wise counselors do not encourage reckless individ-

ualism. Some group habits are essential to any well-organized society. There would be chaos without accepted
modes of behavior. Prisons are filled with noncon-
formists. On the other hand, conformists have stayed
the hand of progress and perpetuated injustice.

Great men and women have never been merely
echoes. Every reform was once an opinion of a person
of conviction, courage, and action. True prophets are
often immediately wrong but ultimately right.

American history has its gallery of heroes and hero-
ines, men and women who have not run with the crowd,
but have shown the crowd a new way. They have con-
fronted Procrustes in his own den, and refused to be cut
down or stretched to size. They remained whole people,
not figureheads or pawns of society.

Ralph Waldo Emerson was one. His essay on self-
reliance deserves constant re-reading: "Envy is ignorance—imitation is suicide. Whoso would be a man
must be a nonconformist. It is easy in the world to live
after the world's opinion; it is easy in solitude to live
after our own; but the great man is he who in the midst
of the crowd keeps with perfect sweetness the independence of solitude."

The Apostle Paul offered the wisest counsel of all:
"Don't let the world around you squeeze you into its
own mold, but let God re-mold your minds from within,
so that you may prove in practice that the plan of God
for you is good, meets all his demands and moves
towards the goal of true maturity." (Romans 12:2.)

Disaffiliation

LL WHO THRILL to the use of clear and forceful language in the service of humanity rejoiced in the persuasive pen of Norman Cousins. When he died November 30, 1990, he had written fourteen books, hundreds of magazine articles, given countless speeches and lectures, and had been awarded more than a hundred honorary degrees.

Norman Cousins' writings will be read for years to come, for they are timeless in their insights. A term in one of his books fell into the web of my mind and stuck. He asserted that one of the dominant moods of our society is the Mood of Disconnection.

Men and women, harried and hurried, feeling the mounting pressures of life, frustrated by problems for which they have neither time nor answers, seek relief by severing their connections with the larger world around them. They drop out and try to live in isolation from other individuals, groups, or institutions.

This isolation has prompted Dr. Jeffrey Hadden, a sociologist at Tulane University, to title this "The Private Generation," based on results of his interview of two thousand University students.

The majority of those interviewed were giving themselves to what the processor called *personalism*—withdrawal from institutions and organizations into themselves, and the rejection of any meaning or authority outside of themselves.

As indicated by Norman Cousins, it is not just students or the young who are exercising the option of disconnection or disaffiliation with anything that would infringe on private liberties, or make claims on time, energy, or resources.

In the lives of many, young or old, disaffiliation is the order of the day: students dropping out of sororities, fraternities, clubs, and churches; citizens of all ages dropping out of communal enterprises, the church, and the political scene by not voting or involving themselves in government in any way.

All who live busy lives can understand why some get fed up with too much organization. It's meetings, meetings everywhere and not an hour to think. So much activity can be frustrating, debilitating, and even fatal. We remember hearing of the grave marker:

> *Here lies Gregarious, the joiner*
> *He clubbed himself to death.*

However, disconnection is not the answer. It is a matter of balance. We all need connections—people, churches, and organizations to which we have loyalties. We are not meant to be alone. Individuals never find their highest fulfillment apart from relationships, and worthy causes and groups languish for lack of participation.

A lonely child, wanting companions, once said to his mother, "I wish that I were two little puppies, so that I could play together." That childish remark is profound. No one is entire in himself. Our families and our friends are the rest of us.

Thomas Mann, a 1929 Nobel Prize winner, said it this way: "It is hard, indeed, without companionship, to have faith and undeniable that actions which proceed from an entirely private and single belief have easily something unbalanced about them."

A person is not likely to be as effective and rational if he always acts unilaterally and in isolation from the checks and balances that come from other people. When we examine any human greatness, we always find it consists of human spirit giving self to a cause, principle, or person. There is no heroism that is not self-surrender.

The sight of people surrendering and submitting to unworthy ends is all too familiar. They harness themselves, right, and left, to alcohol and lust, to vanity and pride, to avarice and covetousness, to stray whims and caprices, to quacks and charlatans, to demagogues and dictators. These are human primal emotional drives for connecting gone wrong. The cure is not in the elimination of the drive, but in its redirection.

The beauty of commitment to a worthy master means that we are set free. Only as we follow that which we can revere do we escape from the irritating slavery of our lesser selves. Great religion goes to the heart of the

matter when it calls for self-surrender and commitment
to the Highest, praying:

> *Make me a captive, Lord.*
> *And then I shall be free*
> *Force me to render up my sword*
> *And I shall conqueror be.*

Remembering

RACTICALLY EVERY CIVILIZED country has set apart days on which to honor its illustrious sons and daughters. In America, we commemorate the sacrifices of those who fought and died to win and preserve our freedom. At times, this has been responsible for mere oratory, full of sound and fury, but in the main, it is highly commendable.

We cannot honor enough the courage and commitment of those who gave their lives in service to our country, But commemoration is not enough. The words of Lieutenant Colonel John McCrae, who died in battle in France on January 28, 1918, in World War I, need to be remembered in each succeeding generation:

> *To you, from failing hands, we throw*
> *The torch; be yours to hold it high.*
> *If ye break faith with us who die*
> *We shall not sleep, though poppies grow*
> *in Flanders Fields.*

We commonly praise freedom as the essence of our

democracy. Yet freedom, per se, is not a virtue. Dr. Harry Emerson Fosdick points out that freedom is a curse when it is not accompanied and balanced by intelligent, responsible personal character.

There are people we dare not set free—dangerous criminals and irresponsible egoists motivated by greed, who think only of themselves, and not the common good. A lesser stress on liberty and more responsibility, kindness, love, and integrity are the greatest expression of freedom and are the highest honor we can pay to those who won our liberty for us.

In recent years, we have enlarged the scope of our remembrances to include people beyond the battlefield, people of achievement in letters, statecraft, art, invention, and in many other areas of human betterment.

It would be hard, indeed, to overestimate our debt to preceding generations. We are the heirs of all the ages. The blessings of modern life are due to the toil, the sacrifice and vision of those who blazed the trails ahead of us in countless fields of endeavor. We stand on the shoulders of giants, and we are the beneficiaries of the work of millions who, though unheralded and unknown to us, have made significant contributions to our lives.

On Memorial Day, we remember, too, the members of our own families who have died. Many place flowers at the graves of loved ones, and remember the years of life and love that were shared. All people have reason to be for the good they have inherited from their ancestors.

The story is told of a famous English statesman who took his son into the family portrait gallery and said: "My boy, you must hear these people speak." And pointing to the various portraits, he continued, "This one says, 'Be true to me.' That one says, 'Be true to yourself.' Here is one who says, 'Be true to your home.' And this one of my mother says, 'Be true to God.'"

We all have a spiritual ancestry. The prophets and seers, and the biblical scholars, have laid the foundations upon which our faith has been built. We owe an unpayable debt to those who have given us a clearer vision of God and interpreted religion in loving and intelligent ways. Again, we are heirs. We are heirs of those who have translated and preserved the manuscripts that guide and undergird our faith.

Think of the debt we owe to John Wycliffe and William Tyndale, who gave us our English Bible. Wycliffe was a fourteenth century professor at Oxford, and one of the greatest scholars of England. He made a complete translation of the Bible from Latin into English. A little more than one hundred years later, Tyndale, even more brilliant, made a new English translation from the Greek and Hebrew. Both men suffered persecution. Tyndale was condemned as a heretic, strangled and burned at the stake.

Each person we remember has a message to us. The great battles of humanity have not yet all been fought. The contributions have not yet all been made. Each generation has its own responsibility and its own challenge. What has been accomplished is but a prelude to what is yet to be done. Goethe says, "He only gains and keeps his life and freedom who daily conquers them anew."

What has been won for us can be lost by careless indifference, ingratitude, or frivolity. The memory of the priceless gifts which have come to us from those of other generations is in itself a call to make our contribution to the betterment of the world that is to be.

Cynicism a Sin?

ENRY STIMSON, A respected Cabinet member in both Republican and Democratic administrations earlier this century, said, "The only deadly sin I know is cynicism."

The early church fathers listed other deadly sins as well, but Stimson had a point when he included cynicism among the dark demons that tempt the human spirit.

Webster defines a cynic as one who is "contemptuously distrustful." Such a mood of contemptuous distrust hangs heavy on our country. Scandals such as the Iran-contra controversy and the Savings and Loan debacle have sharply intensified the crisis in credibility that began with Watergate.

During the Watergate affair, Dr. Kingman Brewster, president of Yale, delivered the university's baccalaureate address, in which he said, "When my contemporaries ask me, 'What is the impact of the Watergate scandal on the young?,' I have to reply, 'Very slight—they are not surprised.' Their basic response is, 'What would you expect?' If I were to characterize what I believe to be the greatest threat to the moral capacity of this nation, I would call it the devolution of declining expectations—which I interpret to be a close cousin to cynicism."

That speech could be made again today. Young and old have lost faith. They are asking, "What can you expect? Who can you believe?"

We are living in a climate of cynicism that is the worst pollution possible. It hangs over us and threatens to envelop us like a thick fog in which we see nothing, do nothing, hope nothing, and, in fact, think nothing can be done. Such cynicism can destroy our nation as readily as enemy bombs.

I am not unaware of our nation's problems but, for many reasons, I do not care to align myself with the cynics of our society. Cynicism has a sorry record of accuracy. Its batting average is low, and it often strikes out.

The theologian, Harry Emerson Fosdick, said, "Cynics always start out by posing as hard-headed wise men, and they always end up being proven soft-headed fools."

Cynicism feeds on generalities and overlooks important particulars.

Listen to the cynics and see how they deal in group judgments: "All politicians are crooked." "All church members are hypocrites." "All young people are irresponsible." Finding one flaw in a group, they condemn the whole. Such assessments are inaccurate and unfair.

When I was in seminary, I read Sinclair Lewis' novel, *Elmer Gantry*, which is the portrayal of a charlatan—a wolf in shepherd's clothing. Lewis knew a cleric who was the fact behind the fiction. But cynics were quick to conclude that Elmer Gantry was typical of all preachers, and that none of them could be trusted.

Undoubtedly, there was a real Elmer Gantry, but there was also an Albert Schweitzer, a George Buttrick, a Harry Emerson Fosdick, a Ralph Sockman, and countless other unknown clerics whose intellectual honesty and moral integrity made them towering figures, both in the pulpit and outside it. Cynics have made dire predictions concerning the church. In the eighteenth century, Voltaire said the church was a dying institution and would not last fifty years. Fifty years later, the house in Paris where Voltaire had made that prediction was being used as a center for distributing the Bible.

Frequently, cynics and skeptics foretell the funeral of organized religion, but the cynics die and are buried, and the church goes marching on.

The cynics said we would never get rid of slavery, and never have public schools. The cynics said that man could never fly in an airplane. Remember the response of a Dayton, Ohio, newspaper editor, when he was informed of the first flight of the Wright brothers, who were natives of Dayton. He said, "I don't believe it. Nobody's ever going to fly. And even if they did, it wouldn't be anyone from Dayton." Now that is cynicism!

But cynicism seldom has the last word.

Several years ago in March, I was aboard an early-morning flight leaving Sea-Tac airport. It was a miserable morning, cold, dark, and dreary. The rain pelted, and the wind blew, but the plane took off. At first, we were enveloped in the clouds. Then, wonder of wonders, within ten minutes after take-off, we were above them looking down on a pure white cotton-puff blanket and up into an incredibly beautiful, clear-blue sky. I cannot remember ever being aware of such a sudden and complete contrast.

I thought to myself, "Minutes ago, you were thinking only of the miserable morning, and now you are glorying in the sheer beauty of the day."

Isn't that like life? We can be at the brink of cynicism and despair because much that we see is dark and foreboding, then we come into the presence of honorable personalities, into knowledge of a larger whole, and our faith is restored, our hope is renewed.

᠙

LEARNING

New Ideas

NE OF THE chief challenges confronting all of us is to stay alive as long as we live. Life can always consist of a series of rebirths, and it is sad when that rebirth stops somewhere along the way for some who at thirty, forty, or fifty years of age die long before they are buried.

How tragic when our lives are marked not by what we achieve, but by the opportunities we miss: the latent skills that are never developed, the intellectual and spiritual gifts that lie forever dormant, or the antiquated ideas that are acquired early in life and never discarded to make way for a new or better philosophy.

On March 25, 1952, Arturo Toscanini was eighty-five years old. That week he rehearsed beginning at 9:00 a.m. with afternoon session from 2:30 to 7:00 in the evening. The day after his birthday, he remarked that it had been fifty years since he first conducted Beethoven's Ninth Symphony, "and I am still far from getting it."

Among the important works of Augustus Saint-Gaudens, famed sculptor, was his statue of Lincoln, now in Chicago's Lincoln Park. Saint-Gaudens was asked if this was not his greatest work. "My next work," replied the great sculptor, "is always my greatest."

Life's real artists never believe they have "arrived." Those who gloat over their victories are the amateurs. True pros believe their best is yet to be.

The story is told that while Socrates was in prison, awaiting his death, he heard someone sing a difficult lyric by the poet Stesichoros. Socrates begged the singer to teach him the lyric. when asked why he he wished to learn it, the great philosopher replied, "I want to die knowing one thing more."

In his book *Love*, Leo Buscaglia tells of a practice in his early family life that has continued to influence him to this day. His father had ordained that no one could come to the evening meal each day without being able to tell of some new thing he or she had learned that day.

"Often," said Buscaglia, "en route to the dinner table, I scurried to the encyclopedia to search out some fact that I could share with the family that evening. Even now, I dislike going to bed without being able to think of some new thing I have learned that day."

A common ailment of our day is premature formation of opinion. Some of us have lived long enough to know that it is important to take a second look at what we believed so readily at first glance. The years teach much that the days never know. Many start out intent on discovering the world of truth, but they settle down on the first little island of knowledge, build a fortress and shoot down any new idea that threatens their security.

It is difficult to let go of any idea that is firmly

believed—often more painful than having a tooth pulled—and there is no spiritual Novocaine available.

Dr. Richard Niebuhr, one of American's greatest teachers of preachers, continually told his students to keep abreast of modern scholarship throughout a ministry. "We must learn to live," he said, "not only on tenets, but tentatives, as well. Ours is an age of ferment, not cement."

It also is always a tragedy when a person's mind moves forward in certain fields for life and work but leaves the religious and spiritual life pegged at a point far behind the person's total experience. "It is a shameful thing," said Marcus Aurelius, "for the souls to faint in the race of life while the boy still perseveres."

A doctor said to his minister, "Why should I go to church? I learned the Ten Commandments and a lot of Bible stories when I was a boy. Why do I need to go and hear all that stuff again?" Suppose he read no professional journals, attended no seminars or clinics, studied no books because he once went to medical school. We surely would not like to have such an out-of-date and out-of-practice surgeon operate on us.

When a mind stops growing, we are not physically aware of any pain. Probably nothing physical aches. In fact, a conscience that ceases to grow suffers not a twinge. Like the hardening of the arteries, the hardening of the heart might progress painlessly until the damage is revealed by a paralyzing stroke (If sin means "missing the mark," as the Greek word for sin implies, then failure to grow is a sin).

The Apostle Paul had one of the keenest minds in

the history of Christendom. His letters still instruct us.
Yet he never felt that he had achieved all that he desired
to do and be.

Paul's letter to the Christians in the city of Philippi
contains a philosophy for all:

> It is not as though I had already attained, or were
> already perfect, but this one thing I do: forgetting
> those things which are behind, and reading forth
> unto those things which are before, I press toward
> the mark for the prize of the high calling of God in
> Christ Jesus.

∾

Cherish the Good

KNOW ALL OF my habits are not worthy of emulation, but some of the ways I have tried to live
my life have been so fulfilling that I do not hes-
itate to recommend them enthusiastically.

For instance, I seldom go anywhere without a pencil and a small note pad. I have long since learned that
a short pencil is better than a long memory. When I
think of something I know I should do, I jot it down. I
record worthwhile thoughts that come to me as I walk
and, when I think it's worth recalling, I write down what
others say.

In gathering material for talks or sermons, I always
write on note paper everything I think I might one day
want to share. This way, I don't have to remember what
it was I wanted to remember. I simply have to try to
remember what I did with the paper I wrote it on!

In more than fifty years of preaching, I have avoided
using notes or manuscripts, but I have seldom ventured
into a speech or a sermon without having written it all
out.

A speaker, if he is wise, does not depend on the

inspiration of the moment. There is a Scripture verse that says it will be given you at that hour what to say. I've never taken much stock in that. I remember too well the woman who described her minister by saying, "He had nothing to say, and he said it."

The lesson behind her words is captured in one of those many sayings I've written down: "By failing to prepare we are preparing to fail."

Besides being a compulsive note-taker, I am an inveterate "clipper." When the family is finished with a magazine or newspaper I return to it and clip items I want to retain. I have several treasure chests of "jewels" to which I return again and again for refreshment, renewal, and inspiration.

Over the years I have read newspapers from front to back. I have made a particular practice of reading the "Letters to the Editor" columns. I do it because "public wisdom" has much to say. It is a paralyzing form of elitism to hold that only properly credentialed men and women have any light to shed on the problems of our day.

Marking my books is another habit that has been of inestimable value. If you open a book in my study, you will soon discover what I consider important, for I have marked the pages in a multitude of ways, from question marks to my own observations penciled along the margins.

Though I have visited libraries regularly through the years, seeking information from books too large or expensive for my personal library, I seldom check out a book because I dare not deface it with my scratchings.

I have not hesitated, though, to mark my Bible. The words are sacred but the paper is not. Books are living things to me, companions sharing the deepest thoughts and feelings.

Though I have countless files of notes, clippings, and well-marked books, I count the week lost when I have not memorized at least one thing—a well-turned phrase, portions of a play, a poem, a Scripture verse, a psalm. I cannot always recall what I once learned, but I feel I have never really lost it. It filters into my subconscious and becomes part of the reservoir from which the response to life is drawn.

I never cease to be amazed how often the things I have learned return at an opportune moment to sustain, console, inspire, guide, or restrain. The psalmist wrote, "Thy word have I hid in my heart that I might not sin against thee." (Psalm 19:11)

In a small way, memorization enables us to be walking libraries or Bibles, carrying with us the truths they would reveal. Sara Teasdale was right:

> *Into my heart's treasury*
> *I slipped a coin*
> *That time cannot erase*
> *Nor a thief purloin.*
> *O better than the minting*
> *Of a gold crowned king*
> *Is the safe kept memory*
> *Of a lovely thing.*

Learning to Fail

INTERPRETERS OF THE human spirit, such as John Bunyan, tell us that it is far more common for humans to traverse the valleys of failure than to stand triumphantly on the summits of success. Yet tragically, most of our education, beginning with kindergarten, has been seriously deficient when it comes to preparing us to confront and handle failure. We are part of a culture that fears failure and worships the golden calf of success.

Nowhere is the deep wisdom, justice, and trust of the Creator more apparent than in His so arranging the universe that we can do our own sinning and make our own mistakes. We cannot understand this. We are so dazzled by ideals that we cannot see that the supreme privilege of freedom is the freedom to do wrong—to fail. Take that away and a person becomes non-moral.

Virtue is of account only in one who might have chosen vice. Maturity is an intelligent use of our liberty.

In our own eagerness to make our children successful, we often rob them of the very foundation of success, which is failure. For the truest success is what is left over after a hundred failures. We are so anxious to love, protect, and make our children happy that we take from them the key to happiness, which is the privilege of making themselves and others miserable. We must give them the right to burn their own fingers, bump their own heads, eat indigestible food, and do the whole range of silly and senseless things. A child that is not permitted to fall will never learn to walk.

I saw a father scolding his son unmercifully after the youngster had struck out, swinging at a bad pitch in a Little League ball game. How does he expect the boy to learn except trial and error?

Let a person succeed all the time, and that individual will remain a child—arrogant, egotistical, and unsympathetic with the plight and problems of others.

It would be difficult to think of many things worse than having to live with a person who had never failed. What an unmitigated tyrant and bore he would be.

What unreasonable demands he would make on others. Having never failed himself, he would lack sympathy and understanding in the failures of those about him. When we know the humiliation of failure we become more fit to live with. It is because we sometimes forget the name of a dearest friend at an hour of introduction that we can sympathize with the embarrassment when it happens to another.

"It is better to fail at doing something than to succeed in doing nothing." Courageous souls have believed that old adage and, at the risk of failure, have set out to make a constructive contribution to our world. One of the "failingest" men who ever lived was always trying experiments that didn't work out, Yet we never think of Thomas Edison as a failure. Success is a bright sun that obscures and makes ridiculously unimportant all the shadowy flecks of failure.

A failure may be a blessing in disguise. It may mean a new direction for our lives. A young man started out at West Point, his heart set on being a soldier. He was prevented from going into the military profession because, try as he would, he couldn't grasp the mysteries of chemistry—then a required subject. He said, assessing himself, "If silicon had been a gas, I should have been a major general." Failing at West Point, he dabbled half-heartedly in engineering, and then, finally, went into the field of art. James Whistler's painting of his mother attests to the fact that the chemical wall that prevented his being a professional soldier had a door that led to greater usefulness.

Success in life does not consist in accomplishing everything we set out to do. The quality of mind and spirit that evolves in the tackling of our tasks, especially during our barren moments of failure and disappointment, counts more than outward success. Often a noble failure serves the world as faithfully as a distinguished success. As a tree is fertilized by its own broken branches and fallen leaves, so great souls use their own failures and convert them to useful ends.

∿

Decorated Minds

ELL ME WHAT you like and I'll tell you what you are," wrote John Ruskin. If we know what a people enjoy, we know their tastes, their interests, their ideals. A study of the titles of the books someone takes from a library during the course of a few months opens windows into his innermost mind and heart. The stubs of my checkbook can also reveal where my deepest devotion resides.

Listening occasionally to a neighbor's radio or record collection gives us a decidedly definite knowledge of his tastes—musical and otherwise. The set of the radio dial in the family car reveals which member was last at the wheel. The pictures on the walls of a home reveal a great deal about the inner life of those who selected them. Even the cartoons and clippings on the refrigerator door and bulletin boards in a home can reflect the philosophy that pervades the family who lives there.

My grandmother was obsessed with the importance of using space in her home for displaying proverbs, poems, Scripture verses, bits of humor, and wise sayings.

She maintained that pictures on walls and items on bulletin boards not only reflected tastes, but were teaching opportunities. We remember, she believed, what we see longer than we remember what we hear.

Her own sense of humor and optimistic outlook on life gave credence to her belief that each of us is an interior decorator. We decorate the inner walls of our minds with the things we learn, and thus we become walking libraries. Lining our minds with positive, loving thoughts, she said, is the finest insurance against old age, against the advance of physical disability.

I can remember her saying that no matter how many there may be in a family or how many friends we may have, we are, in a sense, forced to live a lonely life because we have to live with ourselves every day of our lives. How essential it is, then, no matter what our age now is, to furnish the mind in such a way as to be assured that there are attractive and interesting word pictures on its walls.

People are doubly blessed when they take the time and effort to memorize great poems and Scriptures, she believed, for then we take them with us wherever we go. We may not be able to recall at a moment's notice what we once memorized, but it is never really lost. It has settled into the subconscious to become part of the reservoir from which a response to life is drawn.

Proof of the practicality and wisdom of my grandmother's philosophy is the fact that more than sixty years later, I still hold vividly in mind quotations gathered in my many visits to her home in the West Virginia hills. I still see placed on the kitchen bulletin board:

"Cook carefully, serve lovingly, eat joyfully." And, "Every meal shared in love is a feast." In the living room we read, "No matter what, no matter where, it's always home if love is there."

From time to time, a new quotation would appear with its silent lesson from the wall:

Each day comes bearing its own gifts. Untie the ribbons.

Beauty is as beauty does.

Impart your faith without imposing it on others.

Nothing is started until it's begun.

It was there I first learned that humor is a great teacher:

Give some people an inch and they will think they are a ruler.

Plan ahead—it wasn't raining when Noah built the ark.

Scripture verses were always there to lead, direct, and assure us:

They that wait upon the Lord shall renew their strength, they shall mount up with wings as eagles; they shall run, and not be weary; and they shall walk, and not faint. (Isaiah, 40:31)

Come unto me, all ye that labor and are heavy laden,
and I will give your rest. (Matthew, 11:28)

And always by the door as we left her house, we'd,
read:

You can never do kindness too soon, for you never
know how soon it will be too late.

It is better to light a candle than to curse the darkness.

Today comes shining through the years:

It is magnificent to grow old—if only one stays young.

As a child I always believed it, for she personified it.
And now, somehow, I hope I can, too.

Enrichment

RI L. GOLDMAN, a religion writer for the *New York Times,* was granted a year's leave of absence to study at Harvard Divinity School to enlarge his knowledge of religion and hone his skills as a writer. In his account of the year's experience, he tells how startled he was by the first statement heard in the opening class session. The professor surveyed her students carefully, paused thoughtfully, and then said: "If you know one religion you don't know any."

Goldman, who is Jewish, thought he knew his own faith fairly well and knew something of other religions, but he was unprepared for the boldness of his teacher's assertion. In the year of study that followed, he discovered a wider world of religion than he had ever before envisioned and came to see the wisdom of her statement: "If you know one religion you don't know any."

How constructive it would be if all could have such a broadening experience! It would not mean any less love for or devotion to our own faith, but could rescue us from dogmatism, dissolve misunderstandings, and enlarge our appreciation for the religion of others.

Recognizing my own limited and narrow perceptions, I decided to go to the library and read in the Jewish Talmud. I had been introduced to this ancient literature of the Jews while in seminary, but have spent relatively few hours with it in the intervening years.

The Talmud is a treasury of fables and anecdotes of great insight and power. They are not meant to entertain, but are vehicles for instruction, arresting ways of driving home a truth. The Talmud speaks to many themes:

Truth: If you add to the truth you subtract from it.

Children: Never threaten a child: either punish him or forgive him... If you must strike a child, use a string.

Kindness: "When my time comes to die," said the frog, "I shall go down to the sea, there to be swallowed by one of its creatures. For in that way even my death will be an act of kindness."

On Birth and Death: In a harbor two ships sailed; one setting forth on a voyage, the other coming home to port. Everyone cheered the ship going out, but the ship sailing in was scarcely noticed. To this a wise man said, "Do not rejoice over a ship setting out to sea, for you cannot know what terrible storms it may encounter, and what fearful dangers it may have to endure. Rejoice rather over the ship that has safely reached port and brings its passengers home in peace. And this is the way of the world: when a child is born, all rejoice; when someone dies, all weep. We should do the opposite. For no one can tell what trials and travails await a newborn child; but when a mortal dies in peace, we should rejoice, for he has completed a long journey, and there is no greater boon than to leave this world with the imperishable crown of a good name."

I returned from the library rejoicing in these and other beautiful truths and insights I might have missed. Why, I asked myself, do we not learn more from one another? Why do we wall ourselves against the claims of other faiths? Are we so insecure in our own faith that we cannot risk the venture of listening to another? And why do we not cooperate in the commonalities that bind us together—Jews, Moslems, and Christians, for instance?

There are so many similarities. All are monotheistic. All accept one God who has spoken to humanity. All are called "Religions of the Book" because they consider the relation of God to humans has been written in the Bible or the Koran. All consider God creator of humankind and feel therefore that basically all peoples are equal. All consider God to be merciful.

Why, in a world that cries for unity, must we go on stressing the differences, and leave unexpressed the countless ways we could join hand-in-hand to bring in the day of justice, order, and peace for which we all yearn? More and more I believe the oft-quoted words of Norman Cousins are so very true: "The tragedy of life is not what happens to us, but what we miss."

∾

Embracing Uncertainty

N HIS AUTOBIOGRAPHY, *I Like People*, Grove
Patterson, the famous editor of the *Toledo Blade*,
tells about a country doctor who was called to
the home of a farmer friend at two in the morning. The farmer, named John, had suffered an acute
attack of indigestion.

John died. One of John's neighbors, a pious man
who was riding back to town with the doctor, observed
that it was too bad about John.

"But of course," he said, "God took him for a purpose."

The doctor grunted and replied, "God didn't have
anything to do with it. John brought it upon himself by
eating cold pork at midnight."

That man was more than a faithful doctor. He was a
sensible theologian. It is sad but true that many adults
still have an infantile theology. They are in spiritual
rompers, holding fast to childish ideas that ought to
have long since been discarded.

It is no compliment to God to blame God when our
own stupidity or willful violation of God's laws cause

harm. Although often ashamed of shoddy clothes and furniture, people should be far more ashamed of shoddy ideas and shoddy philosophies.

It is better to have no opinion of God than an opinion that is unworthy of God.

Fortunately, many people have arrived at beliefs that are both emotionally satisfying and intellectually defensible.

Yet, I never cease to be amazed at the unbelievable things some people believe. We may smile when we read of a group of Scottish Christians who refused to eat potatoes because potatoes were nowhere mentioned in the Bible, or we may be saddened by the theology of puritan Richard Braithwaite, who hanged his cat on Monday because it had killed a mouse on Sunday.

Piety is sometimes manifested in very strange beliefs and fanatical forms even by many who believe they are simply manifesting "righteous indignation."

I am aware that we preachers are also often to blame for disseminating religious interpretations that cannot stand in the presence of good scholarship and common sense.

A minister can be a surgeon with words whose scalpel can cut either way—either to heal or to harm his patients' spiritual health and life. The preacher whose scalpel is dull or rusty, or whose theology is antiquated or illogical, is guilty of theological malpractice.

It could be that if the church ever dies, the dagger in its back will be the sermon.

President Woodrow Wilson said, "One of the proofs of the divinity of the Gospel is the preaching it has survived." I repent of my own failings and agonize over what I feel are the distortions of others. But I rejoice that I have both heard and read sermons that have enlarged my horizons and undergirded my faith with solid theology.

Unfortunately, I have also read, or heard sermons that seemed to be mere words without wisdom. I listened to one on my car radio some time ago. The preacher was trying to convince his radio congregation that if they didn't share his little island of religious understanding, they would be cast into eternal hellfire.

It did not frighten me that my soul was consigned to hell, because I could not begin to believe what he believed, but it did anger me because he was limiting the infinite love and mercy of God to his microscopic understanding of it. God asks us to play the game, not to keep the score.

Cardinal John Henry Newman wrote wise counsel for all: "It requires a great deal of reading or a wide range of information to warrant our putting forth opinions on any serious subject; and without such learning, the most original mind may be able indeed to dazzle, to amuse, to refute, to perplex, but not to come to any useful result or any trustworthy conclusion."

The cause of intelligent faith is often hindered by people who, though sincere and religious, resist new truth. I am not immediately impressed when I hear people described as having the courage of their convictions. So what? A bigot has that. The pertinent question is: "Are they willing to alter their conclusions in the light of new evidence?" Some are not. They have closed minds. They even sit on the lid.

Of course, one should not have such an open mind that everything falls out.

"We open the mind," said G.K. Chesterton, "as we open the mouth, with the hope that we will close it on something solid."

We cannot presume to be able to know more than a fraction of all there is to be experienced. As Thomas Edison said, "We don't know the millionth part of one percent about anything." Unlike Francis Bacon, we cannot take all knowledge to be our province.

It is a mark of maturity to be able to live with uncertainty and incompleteness. Many a religious movement has failed because it demanded certainty about uncertain things and left no room for reticence or growth. A God small enough to be fully known and understood would not be big enough to meet human needs.

A young man asked Daniel Poling, the eminent clergyman, what he knew about God. "Very little," Poling replied, "but the little I know has changed my life."

If God wants us to learn to trust, as children trust a parent, how better teach us to trust except by leaving scope for trust and withholding the larger vision for which our hearts cry out?

God gives only enough glimpses of the person of God and of the purpose God is working out to sustain our faith and make us yearn for the nearer presence and the larger knowledge, which is eternal life.

∞

GROWING

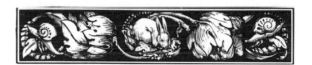

Time for Change

HE RADIO COMEDIAN Bob Bums (The Arkansas Traveler) told of eating Army food for the first time after eighteen years of his mother's deep-fat frying. A week of bland GI fare was enough to cure something that he had never known he had: a life-long case of heartburn.

But rather than feeling relief at the improvement, Bums said he rushed into the dispensary, clutching his stomach and yelling, "Doc, Doc, help me. I'm dying. The fire went out!"

After the shock of the unexpected change wore off, Bums came to realize, as many of us do, that change was for the better.

One of the most difficult changes to which we must adjust is in our physical being. With the passing years our gait is slowed, our waistline expands, muscles become flabby and stairs become steep. Hairlines recede and gray hair appears. The face looking at us from the mirror is not the same face we knew before.

There is a story about a photographer who faced this issue with his best customer. It seems that an attractive young woman had commissioned him to do her portrait once every ten years. Everything had gone well until she was fifty, when she was very disappointed with the proofs and was more than a little indignant.

Charging down to the photographer's studio, she plopped the proofs on his desk. "This picture is not nearly as good as the one made ten years ago," she said, angrily. The photographer looked at the proofs, shook his head thoughtfully for a few seconds, and then nodded sadly, "Well, ma'am, I'm not the man I was ten years ago."

The Apostle Paul had the right outlook on our physical deterioration. His philosophy is revealed in his second letter to the Corinthians: "Though our outward man perish, yet the inward man is renewed day by day. We look not at the things which are seen, but at the things which are not seen: for the things which are seen are temporal; but the things which are not seen are eternal."

God is in the business of bringing about change. God's work of creation could never have happened by staying with the chaos of unformed worlds and an unplanned universe.

There is a hymn which contains the words: "The changes that are sure to come I do not fear to see." That, I suspect, is another one of the falsehoods in which hymn-singing often involves us, for what most of us fear more than anything else in the world are precisely the changes that are sure to come.

Somehow we must deal with change, for change is inevitable. The mere process of growing up—through childhood, adolescence, youth, early adult life, middle age, and old age—with its constant demand for practical and emotional adjustment, makes plain the fact that we need to learn how to deal with it in commonsense ways. Father Time is a tailor specializing in alterations. Change is a given, but wise growth is a choice.

Part of human nature resents change, loving equilibrium, while another part loves novelty, the excitement of newness and change. There is no formula for this tug-of-war, but it is obvious that the absolute surrender to either of them invites disaster. We can't sit on the lid of progress. If we do, we will be blown to pieces.

For some reason we begin to think as we grow older that things in the world will stabilize and life will find an even keel. We think that changes will be fewer and less radical and we will be able to settle back into a comfortable state of living in which most of the things which happen will be somewhat predictable.

Then comes the day when we realize that this kind of plateau in life just will not come, and even if it appears to have come, its stay will be very brief.

The Chinese have a wonderful philosophy in their symbol for the word *change*. It is made up of two characters standing side by side. The character on the left stands for *danger*. The immediate reaction most people have to change is danger—discomfort threat, jeopardy to life as it now is. The character standing on the right is *opportunity*. So, linked to the immediate perception of change as danger is that of a new opportunity.

This is exciting and renewing and the way life should be lived.

God is still bringing about creative things from the changes that come. God can, and does, control changes for the good. Our opportunities come by the continual faith that knows that in every change are the seeds of possibility for good we had not known before.

Ageless

ECENTLY, I RECEIVED a beautifully written letter from a friend in California. He is ninety four years old. His hand is gracefully legible, and the letter contains great clarity of thought. As I placed it in my files, I thought again how sad and unfair it is that old age is so often misinterpreted that we cloud it with prejudices and negative assumptions.

There is a common misbelief that aging means all activities cease, that the brain dries up and muscles shrivel, and that ambition, creative desires, and pleasures vanish into thin air. The aged are often considered the inescapable victims of human decline. It is an unfortunate conclusion and at wide variance with the facts.

The majority of the elderly in our country live rich and full lives. Limited finances and some discomforting ailments do begin to appear, but most older people are remarkable, tough and resilient, and meet life with perspective and humor.

An eighty-three-year-old friend is such a person. He told me he knew he was getting older when it took longer to rest than it did to get tired. "At eighty-three," he says, "a fella may have as much on the ball as he ever had, but it does take more time to get the ball rolling."

It is a mark of ingratitude to resent growing old. There are those who have been denied the privilege. I think of a host of my colleagues, friends and family members who died at an early age and never knew the joy of a long life. Ashleigh Brilliant, whose capsule wisdom illumines issues of the *Seattle Times,* said, "Don't be sad that you have suffered. Be glad that you have lived."

Our American youth cult has created the silly concept that in youth alone is beauty, excitement and achievement to be found. But the joys of youth are often better in retrospect than they were at the time. "The carefree days of youth" is really a misnomer. "Thank God," said Rudyard Kipling, "we never have to suffer again as we did when we were young."

Every stage of life has its difficulties, and each age its compensations.

We do not automatically move from one stage to the next. We become what we are over a long period of time. The thoughts we entertain and harbor write their names on our faces. A beautiful face at five is an accident of nature, but a beautiful face at fifty is a work of art.

Happiness in the latter years of life demands some preparation beforehand. An assured income is not enough with which to meet old age. We must accumulate friends and nurture family ties. We must lay up reserves of mental pleasure. We must plan and work, through exercise and good eating habits, for the health that is important to enjoyment of the later years.

A seminary professor in Chicago tells his students to work with such diligence that they will be prepared to do their best work after they are fifty. David Starr Jordan, the first president of Stanford, believed that his most productive years were between the ages of sixty and seventy, and Bertrand Russell, the humanist, was leading causes for peace in England when he was in his nineties.

It is said that Lady Astor, the first woman to serve in the British Parliament, and a strong supporter of the rights of women and children, dreaded the day when she would be eighty. She thought she would no longer be able to do the things she liked to do. But when she arrived at eighty, she said she no longer wanted to do them.

Common sense accepts the changes of time and appreciates the measure of health and well being that is ours at each stage of life. Adela Rogers Saint Johns, one of America's great writers, knew how to do that. She made the most of each day until her death in 1988. She accepted and laughed at what she called the "ravages of time." Quoting Mark Twain, she said, "Wrinkles should merely indicate where the smiles have been." Advancing years do not need to mean an unproductive life.

In Richard Bach's helpful book, *Illusions*, we read, "If you think your mission in life is over and you are still alive—it isn't." Usefulness in old age may not be confined to spectacular contributions, but to a cheerful outlook and acts of love and kindness that are the best part of all good lives.

The meaning of it all may be best illustrated in the story Thomas Drier tells about seeing an eighty-year-old planting a peach tree. "Why are you doing that?" he asked. "You'll never be around to eat them." "True," said the planter, "but I've been eating peaches all my life from trees I didn't plant, and I'm just trying to repay a little."

～

Seeing the Light

 NE OF LIFE'S greatest treasures is the possession of a religious faith that is embraced by both the heart and the head. Well-ordered beliefs serve as an inner gyroscope that makes steadiness possible in a world of turbulence and rapid transition.

Building a sound theology or way of thinking about God and life is not an easy assignment, for though there are many fine reliable teachers and preachers, there are also charlatans who indoctrinate with conclusions not easily substantiated by the best scholarship.

The learning process involves not only the selection of rational ideas but also the rejection of half-baked, trendy theologies dished out daily by short-order theologians who are always ready to cook up something "special" in response to the social problem of the month.

It is never easy for a serious-minded person to discard deeply entrenched convictions. It is the mark of courage and humility to be willing to let go of what has long been believed if a better thought comes to light. No one leaves school completely equipped with the best view of every conceivable subject. Cocksureness is generally an evidence of limited horizons.

One Sunday morning, a college student whom I knew well heard a preacher express several ideas in biblical interpretation that were different from those the student had been taught in Sunday School in his home town. The student was highly indignant and critical of that preacher, and resolved never to attend that church again.

Years later, when he knew the preacher's view was one accepted by the best biblical scholarship, he remembered his youthful indignation with a sense of embarrassment and chagrin. I know this to be a true report, for I was that college student.

In spite of my early indignation, I was fortunate enough to realize, as a college student, that I had much to learn, and to know in my heart that I did want to grow in my faith. So I took every opportunity in college and in seminary to learn. I prayed daily to seek to know God's will and to walk in God's way, made known, or to be made known to me, and as I grew older. I prayed to escape the mental and spiritual hazards of the stagnation which can come with middle age.

Why is it that as we grow older we are reluctant to grow any other way—to change our ideas and to accept new insights? The justification for conservatism is the desire to preserve the truths and standards of the past.

The dangers of conservatism—of which we are seldom aware, is that in preserving those values, we may miss the infinitely greater riches that lie hidden in the future.

The borders of the empire of truth are not fixed for all time. Each generation must face the adventure of the unknown. Each life must do some exploring of its own. No one can live on borrowed faith and life is a series of rebirths, not just one. It is a pity to die before we are ever fully born.

The humility of Will Durant is worthy of emulation. He said, "Sixty years ago I knew everything; now I know nothing. Education is the progressive realization of our ignorance."

The time came when the old red brick building that was Grand Central Station in New York City became inadequate.

The growing tides of life it served required that it be replaced by something greater. What to do? Stop the trains from running or shift the depot elsewhere? That was not feasible or possible. There was only one thing that could be done. The old building had to be demolished and the new one built around and over it while the immense coming and going of trains continued uninterrupted.

The tens of thousands of railroad travelers went through temporary passageways of rough planks, plaster and dust, noise and confusion. But people could take those inconveniences in good grace because they knew that destruction was a necessary condition to something finer that was being built.

So it is in all spiritual growth. We can accept the uncomfortable process of having our outgrown ideas broken up if we see that the end will not be a lessening of our spiritual life, but a creative enlargement of it.

The greatest need of our day is for a combination of open-mindedness, which makes for progress, with loyalty to convictions which conserve the best contributions of the past.

We must have a union of clear thinking with devotion to worthy and enduring values. We can easily understand and forgive a child who is afraid of the dark. The real tragedy is the adult who is afraid of the light.

Are You Growing?

N MANY HOMES where there are children, you can often find a wall where the height of each child is measured on each birthday. It is interesting to see how much growth has occurred in one year.

As important as knowing how tall we are is somehow to be able to measure our person—the height, width, and depth of our spirit.

Spiritual growth has to do with life, love, and character development. It is more than memorizing Scripture, saying lengthy prayers, or even attending church regularly. While these are important and may contribute to spiritual growth, they are not ends in themselves.

There can be no lines on a wall to mark spiritual growth, but there are questions that, when answered honestly, give us some sense of the direction in which we are moving:

- Do I have a greater awareness of God than I had earlier in my life? The mere passing of time does not necessarily mean we grow spiritually.

* Have I changed my mind recently? This test applies to cherished, long, and deeply held convictions as well as to beliefs and conclusions on social issues. New occasions teach new duties.

  The Apostle Paul offered wise counsel for spiritual maturity:

  > Be not conformed to this world, but be transformed by the renewing of your minds, so that you may discern what is the will of God—what is good and acceptable and perfect. (Romans 12:2)

* Am I seeking answers to any new questions? It is characteristic of a person who is growing spiritually to find from time to time that old answers no longer satisfy and more information is sought. Our opinions become fixed at the point where we cease asking questions.

* Does my life reflect the joy that my religious faith should bring? It is possible to get into religion without having religion get into us—at least get into us enough to transform us into persons with a positive, joyful outlook. "A sour godliness," said John Wesley, "is the devil's religion."

* Do I have any new problems? To be alive is to have problems. But the deeper implication of this ques-

tion is, Do I feel the problems of others? For some, it is not a problem that many are unemployed, homeless, hungry, imprisoned, poor, or ill. They don't care what happens as long as it doesn't happen to them.

* Do I live each day with an attitude of gratitude? Late in his life, G.K. Chesterton, the great English author, set himself the task of defining in one sentence the most important lesson he had learned. He concluded that the critical thing was whether he took things for granted or took them with gratitude. The Scriptures say, "In all things give thanks." (1 Thessalonians 5:18)

* Have I overcome any needless worries?
    The worry cow would have lived 'til now
    If she hadn't lost her breath
    She thought her hay wouldn't last all day
    So she mooed herself to death.

* Do I do something for someone else each day, at some cost to myself? The spiritually mature are always ready to surrender some of their own comfort to provide for others.

* Do I harbor resentment and grudges or am I always ready to forgive?

* Do I have any unfinished tasks? Our society does encourage us to solve, wrap up, and dispose of our

problems neatly. This is supposed to give us a feeling of virtue for having completed our task.

But "finished" does not describe spirituality. The work of the spirit is never done. Our spirituality is a process, never ending a call for continuing growth in this world and into the next.

Healthy Discontent

AVE YOU HEARD the little verse that goes:

Happy am I, from care I'm free
Why aren't all people contented like me?

I do not know how many are as contented as the one who wrote that verse, but many seem to wish to be. More than most anything else in life, most human beings seek contentment.

Countless sermons have been preached on the well-known text from Paul: "I have learned in whatsoever state I am, therein to be content."

And yet, most of us find contentment a difficult state to achieve. It always seems as though there were something lacking, no matter how fortunate we may appear to be.

Before we become unduly critical of unrest and dissatisfaction, it is good to know that discontent has positive meanings and uses. Intelligent and healthy discontent is not a mean and petty complaining over inconveniences.

Intelligent and healthy discontent concerns itself with personal shortcomings and social injustices.

Sensitive people are aware that the world was not designed for contentment. They see too much to challenge them, too much important work to be done, too many necessary changes to be made.

Happily, there are plateaus of contentment when humans may bask in the joy of an accomplishment. Savor that hour and enjoy it. But those concerned with growth do not desire to remain on that plateau.

Permanent contentment leads to stagnation, and whenever we meet a completely satisfied individual, we can be certain there is something wrong somewhere, for the great characteristic of all normal and healthy human beings is discontent.

Discontent is the mainspring of civilization. The greatest reason for the progress of the world since primitive times is discontent. Our great scientific achievements, our great mass of knowledge and learning, in fact, the progress of the centuries in every field of human endeavor, has been brought about by women and men who were unwilling to accept the status quo.

Progress has come from those who longed for change and were willing to dedicate their lives to forsake their own comfort and peace, for the advancement of civilization and the achievement of peace and excellence.

Discontent can act as a spur. Michelangelo's greatness lay in his discontent with himself and his work. Like all the greats of this earth, such as Beethoven and Bach, Rembrandt and Goya, Michelangelo was of such mighty stature that he always believed the best was yet to be.

The tragedy of contentment is greatest in the greatest of all creations—a person. To lose the tension of a restless dissatisfaction with what is, to lose the vision of what might be, to cease to fight the moral battle required to sustain that vision and run up the flag of capitulation, is to lose life itself.

Phillips Brooks said it well (and I have edited his words to include both genders):

> Sad will be the day for all people when they become absolutely contented with the life they are living, with the thoughts they are thinking, with the deeds they are doing, when there is not forever beating at the door of their souls something larger, which they know they were meant and made to do, because they are still, in spite of all, the children of God.

The charge is sometimes brought against Christianity that it is an opiate and lulls people into false satisfaction with themselves. Unfortunately, this is sometimes true. But the message of Jesus was never intended to make people self-satisfied, self-righteous, and completely contented.

Paradoxical as it may seem, the peace Jesus came to bring was an inner stability and power—a peace that still can be possessed by the person who is discontented.

Jesus came to change people and make them realize their own worth and their own responsibility to themselves and to others. To do this, he had to make people dissatisfied with the injustices of the world in which they lived. With all of the great prophets of history, Jesus taught that the good life is a ceaseless quest.

The difference, however, between what Jesus taught and the restless unhealthy discontent of today often comes from our present-day preoccupation with the attainment of material possessions—a distortion (continuously fed by advertisements) of what constitutes a *good life*, and a failure to grasp the concept that the good life must be what is truly good for *all life* on this earth.

COPING

Leftovers

OST OF US have experiences that in retrospect appear more humorous than they did when they happened. I recall one such experience when our family was living in Lawrence, Kansas. My wife, Leone, was called to Michigan briefly to help care for her ailing father. It was the first time in our marriage that the responsibility of caring for the needs of our four young sons was fully mine.

On the whole, all went well. But at mealtime I encountered some difficulty. Preparing food for the household had not been one of my family responsibilities, but in this emergency, I did what I could.

Sometimes I overdid it. Rumor spread that I worshiped my children, placing burnt offerings before them each day! The rumor was not without foundation. "We love you, Daddy," said the youngest, "but when is Mommy coming home?"

Preparing for each meal was a chore in itself, but putting lure in leftovers was the real challenge. How does one recycle hash in any edible way? What do you do with yesterday's leftover carrots? It was an art my wife had mastered, but I never did make it.

I did come to see in subsequent years in the ministry, however, that dealing with leftovers has ramifications far beyond the kitchen. It pervades the whole of life. At times, we must take what yesterday did to us, or what we did to yesterday, and see what we can make of it today. We often must concern ourselves with the remnants of life. We are forced at times to build on waste places, to reclaim what has been lost, and to deal in some constructive way with what is left of earlier dreams and realities.

History is replete with stories of those who have altered or integrated leftovers creatively and made them attractive and nourishing. To learn of the courage and ingenuity of this inspiring company is heartening to us all.

When General William Booth, the founder of the Salvation Army, went blind, it was his son, Bramwell, who broke the news to him. "You mean that I shall never see your face again?" asked the general. "No," said Bramwell, "probably not in this world." The old man's hand moved across the counterpane until it grasped his son's. "Bramwell," he said, "I have done what I could for God and for the people with my eyes. Now I shall do what I can for God and for the people without my eyes." And he did.

Sarah Bernhardt, the lovely and talented actress, lived in her later years in an apartment high over Paris. An old admirer climbed the many stairs to see her, and asked, breathlessly, "why do you live so far up?" "Dear friend," she replied, "it is the only way I can still make the hearts of men beat faster." She took the leftovers of her beauty and glamour and dealt with them in perspective, with humor.

When Nathaniel Hawthorne was dismissed from his government job in the Customs House at Salem, Massachusetts, he went home in despair. His wife rescued him from total, despondency. She listened to his tale of woe, then set pen and ink on the table, lit the fire, put her arms around his shoulders, and said, "Now you will be able to write your novel." Hawthorne responded to her challenge and wrote *The Scarlet Letter.*

Longfellow's translation of Dante may not in itself impress us. But when we learn the conditions under which it was written, we marvel at its beauty and accuracy. While working in the kitchen of their home, Mrs. Longfellow accidentally set fire to her dress. Longfellow arrived after the fire had begun and tried desperately to quench the flames, but it was too late. Mrs. Longfellow was so critically burned that she died. In the ensuing days, Longfellow began his translation to calm his nerves and occupy his mind. He was determined to turn his pain into constructive channels.

Some situations will never be ideal. It is important to know that success, in God's eyes, is not what we achieve, but what the process of the struggle does to us. Dealing creatively and constructively with leftovers, shattered dreams, and thwarted hopes may well bring finer character, deeper joys and a more useful life than any smooth or carefree experience could have fashioned.

In the last analysis, it is not what happens to us, but what happens in us that supremely counts. Whenever we conquer our own fears, doing with love and courage the thing that we have to do, then, no matter what the results may seem to be at the moment, we are victorious. We are counted as successful in the eyes of God.

In Times of Grief

OMEONE YOU KNOW is experiencing grief—the loss of a loved one—and you want to be of help. How do you do it? Perhaps the fear that you will make matters worse encourages you to do nothing. Yet to say or do nothing may be construed as a lack of caring. It is better to try to do something, fumbling and inadequate though we may feel it to be, than to do nothing at all.

Dealing with death is a part of a clergyman's life. Yet I have often encountered situations in which I was not sure what to say or do. I have, however, gathered some insights that I believe are helpful.

Early in my ministry I called on a friend who had just lost his mother. It was my first call in such a situation and I was not sure that my seminary training had prepared me for that, but I did the best thing I knew. Upon arriving at my friend's home, I expressed my sorrow at the news of his mother's death. Shortly into our conversation, I said, "I did not have the privilege of knowing your mother. Please tell me about her." My friend spoke at great length of his mother's kindness and caring, her sense of humor and devotion to everything good. Afterward, he said to me, "I feel relieved for the first time since my mother died. Thank you for coming, for caring, and for listening." It was a clue for me. Be present. Reveal your caring. Listen.

Don't try to put an emotional straitjacket on one who is grieving from any kind of a loss. It makes it more difficult when friends suggest to those who are grieving that they keep a stiff upper lip or that they not take it too hard. It either sounds like we are minimizing the griever's loss or that he lacks backbone.

Encourage the mourner to use the God-given safety valve of tears to express his grief. Tears are not symbols of weakness. They reveal caring. No two words reveal the compassion of Jesus more clearly than those describing his experience when he visited Mary and Martha at the hour of their brother's death. The Bible says, "Jesus wept."

A visit need not be long. Indeed, long-staying may be a shortcoming. A mourner needs time, too, to be alone.

Soften the feelings of guilt that may be present. A husband may feel he should have been more attentive and loving to his wife. Parents often feel they should have spent more time with a deceased child. Young adults wish they had expressed their love of their parents more.

After the shock of death has lessened and family and friends have resumed busy schedules elsewhere, the need for consolation continues. I remember visiting with a woman many months after her husband died. I asked her what her most pleasant memories were of their life together. She recalled a host of good things that she and her husband had shared. Then she said, "Thanks for asking such a question. Most of my friends never mention my husband's name in my presence, fearing that it will activate grief and provoke tears. But I like to know that he is remembered. I never want to lose my awareness of him, for my memories are part of my healing and joy."

Do some act of kindness. One woman said, "After I had prayed that God would bring solace and comfort to my friend, I prepared a macaroni casserole and took it to her home." There are always ways to help. Run errands, answer the phone, prepare meals, mow the lawn, care for the children, shop for groceries, meet incoming planes or buses, or house relatives. The smallest good deed is better than the grandest good intention.

Do what you can to be helpful, but encourage your friend to soon resume a busy schedule. When grief subsides or passes, it leaves a vacuum unless constructive activities fill the void.

We who know so little of the mysteries of life cannot be expected to have all of the answers relating to death, but by being there with physical presence, a phone call, or a letter, by listening and offering what help we can, we may soften grief for another and share in the healing process.

Fight the Blues

F YOU HAVE experienced mid-winter blues or depression, you are not alone. No normal life is lived on a continuously even keel. Dr. Karl Menninger, the eminent psychiatrist, says that not one in four, but four in four, experience mental illness, depression, and gloomy days at one time or another.

Depression is the oldest known mental disorder. The ancient Greeks knew its anguish and pain. Despite centuries of research, it is still not clear what causes it or why women are more often victims than men. Deep and prolonged depression is more than simply feeling "down in the dumps." It is an illness that needs skilled care. We are not kind to our friends when we suggest cures for ills that are beyond our understanding.

However, despondency has varying depths, and most people, escaping its more dismal morasses, become mired in its shallows. Their moody dejections are not altogether beyond their control, and a resolute tackling of their problems, coupled with common sense, can often bring transforming results.

The mental attitude with which life is viewed is crucial. It can mean the difference between being a victor over depression or a victim of it. As food shapes bodies, so thoughts shape minds and moods. Helen Keller said, "I do not want the peace that passes understanding. I want the understanding which brings peace." That is, to think those thoughts that dispel and displace gloom, and make peace and serenity likely.

Whatever the circumstances, misanthropes will see and emphasize the negative side. Some will even borrow trouble not present. One woman, when asked how she was, responded, "Oh, I feel better, but I always feel bad when I feel better, because I know I'm going to feel worse."

Brave souls do not blame circumstances. Circumstances, however, often are tragic, and make depression inevitable. To be sad in bereavement, disheartened by disappointment, dismayed by the world's greed and cruelty, or disconsolate when personal trust is betrayed is natural. But to deduce from the presence of misfortune the right to be a despondent person is a fatal error.

Said a sympathetic friend, "Affliction does color life." "Yes," said the young woman crippled by paralysis, "and I propose to choose the color."

University of Wisconsin researcher William Morgan confirms the conclusion of countless counselors that exercise can be a simple, but effective, treatment for depression and anxiety. Morgan, who has studied sports psychology extensively, says, "The link between depression reduction and physical activity is so clear that it is no longer even questioned by most researchers."

People who fall victim to occasional depression and moodiness may find some help from those who have conquered it, and from the methods they have used.

The ideal, however, is not, just to be able to conquer our blue moods, but to forestall them with a life that keeps its zest and savor. This achievement involves the whole process of healthy living, from holding great faiths about life's meaning, to enjoying varied hobbies and recreations that diversify life's interests.

Much of the depression we struggle with downstream could have been prevented upstream. Great convictions to live by, great resources to live from, great purposes to live for, the love of nature, the companionship of good books, the nurture of friendship, the fine uses of play—such factors enter into a life that keeps its savor, and they furnish an immunity to despondency which makes cure needless.

∾

The Gift of Humor

HE TIME HAS come to take humor more seriously. The capacity to smile, chuckle, or laugh is one of God's greatest gifts. But unfortunately for many people, the gift of humor lies dormant or underdeveloped. Laughter has a tonic effect. It is an instant vacation—a tranquilizer with no side effects. Norman Cousins calls it "internal jogging."

Laughter exercises and stretches scores of muscles, imparts energy-giving sugar to the body, and suffuses the whole organism with a feeling of well-being. "A merry heart doeth good like medicine; but a broken spirit drieth the bones," says Proverbs 17:22.

In our age of scientific miracles and medical breakthroughs, it just might be that something as simple as laughter is the best medicine after all. Our body politic needs the healing it can bring, for ours is a grim generation.

But it is doubtful if we will soon again, if ever, see the likes of Will Rogers. "I don't make jokes," he said. "I just watch the government and report what I see."

It was because Will Rogers loved our land and its

leaders so deeply that he could poke good fun at both. He was aware that the next best thing to solving a problem was seeing the humor in it.

Humor was Abraham Lincoln's bulwark against the bitter, bloody disasters of civil war. His gaunt, towering figure, clad in a flaming flannel nightgown, used to stalk through the White House at midnight seeking someone still awake to share a funny story he had just read.

"The neigh of a wild horse on his native prairie," we are told, "was not more hearty than Lincoln's laugh."

The great Mohandas Gandhi, a sad man because he lived within the suffering and injustice of the caste system and national turmoil, was also one of the wittiest of men. He was quick to use humor, not because he was irreverent or trivial, but because he was a man of proportion. He possessed the kind of humor that Thomas Macaulay said Joseph Addison had—"a mirth consistent with tender compassion for all that is frail and a profound reverence for all that is sublime."

In the right setting and spirit, humor can break down barriers that separate people. Laughter, the shortest distance between hearts, has rescued many marriages, turned many a tense situation into a creative experience and has even waked dozing parishioners.

It is sad, but true, that religion has often failed to see the great worth of God's gift of humor, and has even impeded it at times.

Perhaps that is because in the eyes of many, laughter is incongruous with worship. Ralph Waldo Emerson's eccentric aunt, Mary Moody Emerson, once scolded a young preacher because she saw him smiling in church. He defended himself by saying, "But I saw you smile, too, Miss Emerson." The old lady replied, "Well possibly you did, but it was a sardonic smile."

There exists an erroneous impression that the determination to improve the lot of humanity is associated exclusively with the somber aspects of life.

In George Bernard Shaw's gripping play, *Major Barbara*, the mother of a young man who has joined the Salvation Army says to the title character in disgust, "Good gracious, Barbara you talk as though religion was a pleasant subject."

Somehow we have managed to interpret God as a celestial Scrooge who peers over the balcony of Heaven trying to find anyone who is laughing or enjoying life in any way, and when he spots such a person, yells, "Cut it out!"

The Bible does not give such a concept of our Creator. "Serve the Lord with gladness: Come before His presence with singing." (Psalms 100:1)

Radiance and joy characterized the life of Jesus. He carried with him a glad contagion that brightened the lives of those about him.

Happily, many of life's choice spirits have not been blind to the relationship of humor to religion. "If you're not allowed to laugh in heaven," said Martin Luther, "I don't want to go there."

Sensitive souls never use humor to make sport of life's unfortunate people. Their humor is never cutting or mean—irony sometimes, but not sarcasm. Neither is their humor derogatory of race, religion, or ethnicity. It is fun without filth and lightness without obscene levity.

It is a mark of wholeness and wholesomeness when our humor is directed at ourselves. When we see our own mistakes and pretensions, it keeps our egos in proper perspective.

"The original sin," said Oscar Wilde, "is that we take ourselves too seriously."

A doctor prescribed for one of his "uptight" patients that he take himself with a grain of salt. It is easy to believe that imagination was given to humans to compensate for what we are not, and a sense of humor was provided to console us for what we are.

∽

Collecting a Life

Y MOTHER-IN-LAW died after having lived ninety-five beautiful years. During the weeks following her death, my wife, her sister, and I spent days sorting, saving, and discarding the letters, pictures, and mementos that she accumulated across her long and useful life. She was a thrifty woman, and it seems there was very little she discarded.

Each closet and dresser drawer has yielded items of great interest—many tracing back to the last century. Her treasures of correspondence and pictures comprised an invaluable collection, linking her with family and friends past and present. It has not been easy to know how to deal wisely and lovingly with each item that had meant so much to her.

That which we receive and keep—the collections we make—can enrich our lives. They also can be an invaluable gift to our children and grandchildren and to others who live after us, who, for various reasons, never knew or have forgotten this necessary bond with the past. Bonding strengthens our lives and it can also strengthen society.

It is both interesting and amazing to read the lists of collectibles published. One person's junk can be another person's prize. But there are collections whose worth is beyond measure to all who collect them. These are the collections of intangibles.

Try collecting something beautiful each day—not something you can put into a drawer, on a bulletin board, or in a scrapbook, but something you can file away in your memory to turn to when things are going badly or to enjoy in moments of quiet.

If you have a collector's eye, you will find all sorts of things: stars moving silently and majestically through the dark of night, tall grass shimmering in the sun, white clouds reflected in a pond, or white sails silhouetted against a blue sky.

There is a wealth of beauty around us each day just waiting to be collected. How sad if we pass heedless and unseeing.

Try collecting smiles. Despite all the improvements in methods of communication, nothing can surpass a friendly smile. Try it just for one day. You will be so pleased with your collection that you will want to keep right on collecting. Of course, to collect smiles you have to smile at others first. Start with the first person you see when you get up in the morning and keep right on through the day.

Sometimes people will not return your smile. Maybe they are too tired, worried, preoccupied, or ill. Maybe they will be so surprised at seeing you smile that they won't respond right away. Don't despair, for usually:

The world is like a mirror
Reflecting what you do
If you smile right out at others
They'll smile right back at you.

If you keep right on trying, sooner or later you'll get some kind of a smile for your collection. Often the one that's hardest to get is the one you will prize the most.

Collect a beautiful sound each day. It could be a soft lap of waves or the bubbling laugh of a child. It might be the high clear sound of a bird or the symphony of insect sounds that we hear only when we are very quiet and listen very closely. Sort out the beautiful sounds from the many noises that jar the ear. Select sounds that soothe the spirit and quiet the nerves. Listen often to great music and discover that the melody lingers on after the stereo has been turned off.

Collect and memorize at least one beautiful thought each day. It may be a verse of Scripture, a stanza of poetry, or a word of wisdom uttered by one of the seers of the day or a day gone by. It may be the thoughtful and perceptive word of a friend.

We never lose what we once knew. All that we learn settles into the subconscious and becomes part of the reservoir from which we draw our response to life.

SAYING

Unspoken Words

HAVE A LITTLE book in my library titled *7,000 Words Frequently Mispronounced.* It is a disconcerting thought to know that every time I stand to give a talk, I have at least seven thousand distinct possibilities of making myself look ridiculous. It is almost enough to encourage a vow of perpetual silence.

There is also the risk of incorrect grammar. Oh, those pronouns! Is it *I,* or is it *me?* And how about sentence structure? A speaker's sentence structure should be one of the proudest things he is of!

I certainly have made my share of these mistakes and others, but what I regret more than the mistakes I have made in public speech or private conversation have been the regrettable silences—not what I have said, but what I have failed to say. These remembered silences—the times when I should have spoken, but said nothing bring more agony than the memory of mispronounced words.

I suspect that I am not alone in my memories of regrettable silences. A friend tells me of a time he has long regretted when he did not defend a friend who was receiving character assassination in a group where the friend's name was being discussed. "I am sorry," he said, "that I did not heed the dictum to defend the absent, but stood quietly by. In my silence, I seemed to give assent to what they were saying."

There are those who do not speak up in meetings where important issues of justice and fair play are at stake. Often, their silence contributes to unwise or unfair decisions. Those who are silent when they know they should speak, feigning agreement they do not feel under the guise of tact, would be more honest if they recognized their silence for the cowardice it is.

Some people trace their silence to the fear that they will be ostracized by others if their opinions are not in line with those of the group. But someone I know once made an interesting observation. He said, "We wouldn't worry about what others think about us if we only knew how seldom they do." In any case, it is indeed regrettable when many of the best observations are reserved for the hallways after the meeting has adjourned.

When we look back in history, we can't help but wonder about regrettable silences. It was gracious and generous of Joseph of Arimathea to give his own gravesite for the burial of Jesus. But where was he when Jesus was on trial? Joseph was described as a respected man. A word from him might have turned the tide.

Martin Luther King Jr. said that when historians write about the 1950s and 60s, they will not accent the riots in Detroit or the strident voices in the Watts District of Los Angeles. They will note the appalling silence of the multitudes of good people who never lifted a voice of protest in the presence of great injustice. ◁ REV. MARTIN NIEMILLER

Sometimes colleagues in business and professional life are not as affirming and supportive of one another as we might assume they would be. The silence of a colleague in the presence of worthy accomplishment by another can contribute to lasting hurt.

An elderly friend of mine tells of an experience he had as a young college professor and lay preacher. He was asked to preach on a special occasion, and he prepared his material with utmost care. Three older preachers sat with him in the chancel when he spoke, and several others sat in the pews. His confidence was at a low ebb that morning, for he was only a youngster in the presence of experienced pros. But he did his best.

At the close of the service, when he needed a few words affirming the worth of what he had shared, no preacher came forth from the pews to greet him, and two of the three ministers who shared the pulpit with him ostentatiously avoided any comment at all. But the third was gracious enough to find something of value in his effort. Those few words of encouragement lodged in my friend's mind for more than five decades. They are remembered to this day for their uplifting power.

There are also regrettable silences in homes where love and affirmation remain unexpressed. The bitterest tears are often shed at gravesites where mourners remember that they neglected to speak their love and gratitude while the dead were alive to hear. While words can hurt, and hurt deeply, the absence of words can hurt still deeper:

It isn't the thing you do;
It's the thing you leave undone
Which gives you a bit of heartache
At the setting of the sun.
The tender word forgotten,
The letter you did not write,
The flower you might have sent
Are your haunting ghosts at night.

Mere Words

MONG THE MANY fascinating and distinguishing aspects of being a human being is the ability to use words to convey ideas.

From the grunts, groans, and signals of primitive humans to the complicated, intricate language pattern that now is ours is an intriguing pilgrimage—journey with no end. The English language has five times as many words it had in the day of Queen Elizabeth I. As new words are being born old words are changing.

When I was a boy, certain kinds of music were described as being *hot*—today the same music is described as *cool*. It used to be that character was something a person had—now it is something he is.

Many good words have passed from popular usage. *Fellow-traveler* was once a fine phrase describing a companion of the journey. But now call one a "fellow-traveler" and there is lifting of the eyebrows. *Comrade*, too, was once a fine word, now call another "comrade" and some see red.   GAY _ _ _

Dr. George Buttrick was one of America's most eloquent preachers. He knew the power of words. In one of his sermons, he told of speaking at a high school commencement. At the bottom of the program he noted the class motto—"Deeds, not words." Dr. Buttrick rebelled at this; words, he reasoned, are deeds. We commonly think that the greatest way in which we can help others is by the giving of tangible gifts of money, food, or clothing. These are positive expressions of caring, but words are gifts too.

Our memories enable us to retain gifts of kind words long after a tangible gift is forgotten or gone. Mark Twain said, "I can live two months on a good compliment."

The tide of battle has turned on the oratorical skills of noted leaders. Early in World War II the waves of Nazism were beating on the shores of England, threatening to inundate that island of millions of people. On June 4, 1940, a bulky tank-like man, whose trademark had become a cigar jutting from his lips like a turret gun on a tank, arose and spoke words of hope and courage to the many who were dispirited and afraid: "We shall fight on the beaches; we shall fight on the landing ground; we shall fight in the fields and in the streets; we shall fight in the hills. We shall never surrender."

They're words, some may say, but they set a tottering nation on its feet and gave hope to millions. Truly Churchill mobilized the English language, enabling it to fight on behalf of peace.

Words spoken or written—like all of God's great gifts can be distorted and used to ends that alienate and divide rather than build community. Friendships have been strained or broken by words. When we were younger we might have returned the taunt of another with, "Sticks and stones may break my bones—but words can never hurt me." That's not true. Another's critical or biting words can hurt us deeply or even endanger our reputations or our jobs. Consider this story:

On a sailing vessel, the mate of the ship, yielding to temptation, became drunk. He had never before been in such a state. The captain entered into the ship's log the record of the day: "Mate drunk today." When the mate read this, he implored the captain to take it out of the record, saying that when the owners of the ship read the entry, it would cost him his post, and the captain well knew this was his first offense. But the unrelenting captain refused to change the record and said to the mate, "This is the fact and into the log it goes."

Some days afterward, the mate was keeping the log, and after giving the latitude and longitude, the run of the day, the wind and the sea, he made this entry: "Captain sober today." The indignant captain protested when he read the record, declaring that it would leave an altogether false impression in the minds of the vessel's owners, as if it were an unusual thing for him to be sober. But the mate answered as the captain had answered him: "This is the fact and into the log it goes."

Rotarians have a four-way test that helps them to determine what they shall say or do. Such criteria are of value to us all:

Is it the truth?
Is it fair to all concerned?
Will it build goodwill and friendship?
Will it be beneficial to all concerned?

Add to these guide posts the wisdom of James Whitcomb Riley's prayer and we have wise counsel for the living of each day:

> *Let me no wrong or idle word unthinking say;*
> *Set thou a seal upon my lips just for today.*

Talking Rot

HEN HAROLD MACMILLAN, former prime minister of Great Britain, was asked about the education policies of his cabinet, he used to quote one of his Oxford professors, a distinguished old scholar who would greet each new class with the same speech on educational philosophy:

> Gentlemen, you are now about to embark on a course of studies which will occupy you for two years. Together they form a noble adventure. But nothing that you will learn in your studies will be of the slightest possible use to you in years to come save only this: That if you work hard and intelligently you should be able to detect when a man is talking rot, and that, in my view, is the main, if not the sole purpose of education.

H.L. Mencken, a caustic commentator on the American scene early in this century, was singularly successful in knowing when others were talking rot. He lamented the fact that most people are like sponges, absorbing all that is said or spoken as true. Mencken wrote:

> We take pride in the fact that we are thinking animals, and like to believe that our thoughts are free, but the truth is that nine-tenths of them are rigidly conditioned by the babbling that goes on around us from birth, and that the business of considering this babbling objectively, separating the truth in it from the false, is an intellectual feat of such stupendous difficulty that few are able to achieve it.

The difficulty of achieving the feat of logical thought should deter no one from the effort. When we use our critical faculties it does not mean we are negative personalities, censorious nit-pickers, unpatriotic, or irreligious. It means we are doing our best to use the God-given intelligence we have.

Ignorance is not bliss. Criticism of another's ideas does not mean that the sincerity of the propagator is questioned or his integrity is impugned. It simply means disagreement with what is believed and articulated.

There are many outrageous distortions and frightening falsehoods around in our world today in the guise of religious truth. They deserve to be unmasked.

The Reverend Richard Butler, a principal leader of the Aryan Nations Movement affirms that he and his disciples are truly God's "chosen people." "God has promised us," he says, "a homeland here in the Northwest." "The U.S. Government," he continues, "through equal rights legislation and court decisions affirming equality, is bent on destroying the white race in America."

The man is babbling rot. He has no logical leg to stand on. The Bible and biology agree that God has made of one blood all nations. Lovers of liberty expect and even urge diversity.

Christian evangelical leaders are using their money, spirit, convictions, and millions of members to battle in the secular arena, and are playing an increasingly influential role in U.S. politics.

It is good that this is so. All have a responsibility to participate. Liberals have been involved for years. However, the religious right goes beyond anything liberals have asserted by claiming to speak for God and by questioning the morality or fitness to hold political office or serve God's will in other ways.

In his book, *Listen America!* the Reverend Jerry Falwell says, "If a person is not a Christian he is inherently a failure." Nonsense. Was Gandhi a failure? Was Rabbi Raphael Levine's contribution to our society of little consequence?

Televangelist Pat Robertson says, "From the biblical standpoint, the rise of homosexuality is a sign that society is in the last stages of decay." Of the Jews, Robertson writes, "When they return to faith it will be the equivalent of the resurrection of the dead."

"The Constitution of the United States," he continues, "is a marvelous document for self-government by Christian people. But the minute you turn the document into the hands of non-Christian people, they can use it to destroy the very foundation of our society." The man may be sincere, devoted, and a Phi Beta Kappa, but he is talking rot.

It is clear that these people want the United States government to stop being neutral about religion. They want to legislate a "Christian Nation" in which all laws and institutions would conform rigidly to their authoritarian set of fundamentalist beliefs. They attack anyone who disagrees with them as "ungodly," "anti-Christian," or "anti-family."

Sir William Osler was right, "The greater the ignorance, the greater the dogmatism." Were the energies that these men expend in defense of dogma transferred to the search for truth, religion and society would fair better in all quarters.

The tasks of social change are for the tough-minded and competent. Those who come to the task with the currently fashionable mixture of passion and ignorance only add to the confusion.

The greatest need of our day is for a combination of open-mindedness (which makes for progress) and loyalty to those convictions that conserve the best contributions of the past.

We must unite clear thinking with devotion to worthy and enduring values.

In the field of religion, we need not more light, but a clearer flame.

Poetry of Life

HERE IS AN old story with a lot of wisdom in it about two cowboys who were snowbound for the winter in the mountains of Colorado. Each had a book which he read continuously. One read *One Thousand and One Interesting Facts*—the other Omar Khayyam.

When spring came, the two traveled to Texas, and both courted the same girl. One would say, "Miss Louisa, did you know that the Brooklyn Bridge is 5,678 feet long?" The next night, the other would draw on his winter's study and say:

> *Here with a loaf of bread beneath the bough*
> *A flask of wine, a book of verse—and thou*
> *Beside me singing in the wilderness,*
> *And wilderness were Paradise enow.*

Need I tell you that Louisa went for Omar?

Valuable as the poetic touch is, it is often squeezed out of life today by the ascendancy of science. Ours is a technological civilization of iron and steel, cranes and levers, buttons and sirens, star wars and clatter. It is a civilization with little time for other than facts.

The ideals of science are rigors of method, insistence on procedure, total objectivity. There is no room in scientific ventures for the poetic, sentimental or romantic—no room for wonder and awe unless you are up in a spacecraft, looking at the Earth. Nothing must remain hidden. To the greatest extent possible, all aspects of life are laid out on the laboratory table for examination, classification, measuring, testing, and retesting.

We have no quarrel with the scientific mind. In fact, there are still areas where it could be used more widely than it is. But we have seen too much of what it does to people when it absorbs, encompasses, and rules the whole of life. The loss of the poetic and romantic from our world is a deadly thing for the human spirit. There is a crying need for more real music, for dance and laughter. The poetry of life is in short supply.

An appalling proportion of Americans seem to be bored to death. No one ever discovers anything out of boredom. And so they buy tranquilizers to shut out the frustration of doing nothing, or the joy of being surprised. They take pep pills to provide a little energy, false interest and excitement, to take away the grayness of the day.

At the other end of the spectrum are the hurried, always trying to get ahead, afraid to stop and watch and listen, chafing at the long lines in the supermarket and forever switching lanes on the freeway. They are indeed prime candidates for ulcers.

An ulcer is an unkissed imagination taking its revenge for having been jilted. It is an unwritten or unread poem, neglected music, an unpainted water-color or an undanced dance. It is a declaration from the person's inner being that a clear spring of joy has not been tapped, and that it must break through muddily and painfully on its own.

G.K. Chesterton reminded us that the meanest fear is the fear of sentimentality. How often it robs life of its best. We laugh when we want to weep. We live on the surface when all the time we want to think and feel from the heart deeply. We hide our tenderness under a cloak of sophistication. It may well be that history will honor its poets and lovers more than its scientists and states-men, for it is they who keep alive what is most human.

> 'Tis the human touch in the world that counts
> The touch of your hand on mine
> That means far more to the lonely heart
> Than shelter or bread or wine
> For shelter is gone when the night is past
> And bread lasts only a day
> But the touch of the hand
> And the sound of the voice
> Sing on in the heart always.

Speak Out

HEN IT WAS first announced that education professor Leo Buscaglia was to teach a course entitled "Love" at the University of Southern California, a few people raised their eyebrows. They didn't consider love a scholarly subject or a serious part of a college curriculum. Many considered it irrelevant. Nevertheless, the class filled quickly, and there have always been long lists of those waiting to enroll.

Interest in Leo Buscaglia and his loving philosophy continues to grow. It is strange that anyone would consider it irrelevant, for the human spirit's deepest need is to be loved. The greatest act of a human being is to meet another at his point of deepest need and love him. But while everyone has the capacity for love, its realization is the most difficult of achievements.

Ashley Montagu, the renowned anthropologist, suggested that the main thrust of education should be to train individuals in the art and science of being a warm, loving human being. It is possible to have a graduate degree and be a walking encyclopedia of knowledge, and still be a cold, uncaring person. It could be argued that our education is a failure no matter what it has done for the head if it has done little or nothing for the heart.

But some of the most loving people find it embarrassing to say endearing things to one another. Even those whose professions require skill in learning and saying loving lines to others on stage or screen can't find the words to say them in real life. Henry Fonda was one. Shortly before his death, he said, "It is only in the last few years that I've been able to say to my children, 'I love you,' and I've loved them since the day they were born."

Fear of sentimentality robs life of its best. Dr. William Stidger, for many years a professor at Boston Theological Seminary, tells of visiting an old Cape Codder who had lost his wife by death. Stidger spoke at great length about her virtues. About two hours later the old gentleman admitted that everything Stidger had said was true: "You know," he said, "I did love her so much that there were certain times when I came near telling her."

A husband may love and respect his wife, but if he never gives voice or visibility to his affection, the romance of their married lives will not remain long. The man, of course, may say, "I don't have to tell her. She knows it." Well, maybe she does, or maybe she doesn't. Or maybe she does, but still wants to be told. How sad if, in keeping silent, the husband denies what would mean so much to both of them. Words without love are sounding brass; but love without words can lose its music.

Yoko Ono, wife of the late John Lennon, is a tough, strong woman. She has held together remarkably well since the assassination of her husband. Theirs was a beautiful love. She was asked, "Was there anything you didn't get a chance to say to John before he died?" "No," she said, smiling, "we said it all, every day throughout our fourteen years together."

So let this be the first day of the rest of our lives. Set forth to say those loving things that need to be said.

Gather ye rosebuds while ye may.
Old time is still a-flying.
And this same flower that smiles today,
Tomorrow will be dying.

—Robert Herrick

DOING

David's Lesson

HE AVERAGE CHILD is not often interested in Sunday School, which is usually endured rather than enjoyed. One boy, however, despite the passage of many years, can still remember vividly when he first heard one of the stories told in Sunday School. It was the exciting and unfailingly interesting story of the battle between the ancient heavyweight champion, Goliath of Gath, and the rising young lightweight, the shepherd boy of Israel, David.

The incident that brought David to the forefront in the life of his people illustrates how a man can make his own opportunities. David was not a member of the army of Saul. He was only a shepherd boy who had left his flocks on the hillside and come down to the camp to bring food to his brothers.

When David suggested that he might fight the Philistine champion, his eldest brother scathingly rebuked him, saying, "Why did you come here? And with whom did you leave those few sheep in the wilderness? I know your pride, and the naughtiness of your heart."

But David secured Saul's consent to allow him to face Goliath, and the king even put his own armor on David, and gave him his sword. Thus armed. David found, as many people also have found, that he could not fight with another man's equipment. With his shepherd's sling and five smooth stones from the brook, David could do what he could not accomplish with Saul's armor and the sharp sword he didn't know how to use.

A person can always fight better with his own weapons. Many people, despising their own aptitudes and powers, have tried in vain to wield the sword of another and have ingloriously failed. The use of apparently inconsequential talent will make its possessor of greater service to humanity than a futile attempt to imitate the ability of someone else. David showed his caliber in having sufficient self-reliance to fight the battle with his own weapons in his own way.

David probably would not have wielded the spear of Goliath any better than the sword of Saul. But he could have gone his way and never fought Goliath at all, for nobody expected much of this shepherd-boy camp follower. If he had done nothing he would not have been blamed, for no one would have known.

But David was a doer and not a maker of excuses. It is not the tool that counts, but the person behind the tool; not the opportunity, but the ability, power, and willingness to use it. The shepherd's sling in the hands of the right man did what the proudest warrior in Saul's army could not accomplish.

Today many sit on the sidelines or in the bleachers

and talk about what they might do if they had greater talents and larger opportunities. One person bewails a lack of wealth, and another a slender ability. Some dream of what they would do if they had a congenial environment or a more powerful position. The slacker, whatever his opportunities or limitations, is always rich in excuses, never willing to acknowledge the cowardice of laziness, which prevents making the effort that is always the price of any kind of achievement.

The person who buries one talent would probably treat ten in precisely the same way. The ultimate challenge is to do the best we can with what we have, where we are, all the time.

> *Bloom where you are planted.*
> *If you can't be a pine*
> *On the top of a hill*
> *Be a scrub in the valley, but be*
> *The best little scrub by the side of a hill...*
> *We can't all be captains, we've got to be crew*
> *There's something for all of us here*
> *There's big work to do and there's lesser too,*
> *And the thing we must do is the near,*
> *If we can't be a highway then just be a trail*
> *If you can't be the sun be a star*
> *For it isn't by size that you win or you fail*
> *Be the best of whatever you are.*

Extend Yourself

URING MY COLLEGE days, I was a physical education major, preparing for a career as a football coach. Therefore, I was in the gymnasium more hours than most students at the school. Perhaps for this reason I have remembered through the years two words printed in extra-large letters on the wall of the gym.

Those words were: EXTEND YOURSELF. That is, do a little more than you can easily do. In this way, you strengthen your abilities and enlarge your skills.

I never would have guessed when these words were first fastened in my mind that they were telling a universal law—the law of the second mile—applicable far beyond gymnasium and physical education students.

We must be willing, and even eager, in all of life, to do more than is expected or required, or we will always be average, mediocre, mundane human beings. The great personalities of history have always been those who extended themselves. They gave more than was expected or required and they were ready to take less than they deserved.

The person who comes immediately to mind is Dr. Wilfred Grenfell, who traveled throughout the Labrador country treating the ills of hundreds of people with a minimum of equipment, and in the most primitive conditions.

Grenfell did what he had to do better than he had to do it. He extended himself. On the outside of his little black medical bag were engraved the words: "Be kinder than necessary."

Who are the great students? Those who do their work thoroughly and go beyond what is assigned. They listen attentively, knowing that a cat-napping, wool-gathering mind is the enemy of learning. Others trudge reluctantly to class and give only half-hearted attention to that for which they pay so much to receive.

They do not drink at the fountain of knowledge—they only gargle.

I have often wished I could be eloquent enough and persuasive enough to go to schools across the land and say to young people, "If any teacher compels you to read a hundred pages, surprise him and read two hundred."

When grades are distributed, it will be difficult for that teacher to keep from giving an *A*. But the *A* will not be the student's chief reward. The joy of learning will be there as well.

It is the extra effort that makes the great athlete. the superior track star runs extra laps to prepare for competition. The great ball carrier, although given only enough interference for a five-yard gain, sets out to make it ten.

At the close of each athletic season, All-Conference,

All-State, All-American, All-Pro teams are selected. Only one question is asked: "What has this competitor done more than others to be singled out for this recognition?"

James J. Corbett, a heavyweight boxing champion of another era, was asked the secret of being a champion. "Fight one more round," was his simple answer. Do more than your opponent.

Extend yourself.

It's the extra that counts in our work. The employee who goes to work each day like a quarry slave scourged to his dungeon, misses the fulfillment that could have been realized by a willingness to do more than is expected or required.

A retired executive was asked the secret of his successful career. He replied that it could be summed up in three words: "And then some."

Abraham Lincoln said those who do no more work than they are paid for are not worth what they get.

Great marriages follow the rule of the "second mile." Happily married couples can throw away their marriage vows, not because they intend to violate them, but because they do not want their love to be confined to the limits of the law.

In Shakespeare's play *Othello*, Iago says of Desdemona, "She considers it a vice in her goodness not to do more than is expected."

Such it is with each partner in a happy marriage.

Extend yourself was a central theme in Jesus' teachings. "You have heard that it hath been said, 'an eye for an eye and a tooth for a tooth,' but I say unto you that you resist not evil, but whosoever shall smite you on the right cheek, turn to him the other also. If anyone will sue at the law and take away your coat, let him have your cloak as well, and if anyone compels you to go with him a mile, go with him two."

"What do you more than others?" Jesus asked. "If you do only what is required of you, you are unprofitable servants. If you salute your brethren only, what have you done? Love your enemies, bless them that curse you, do good unto them that hate you, and pray for those who despitefully use you and persecute you."

To thus extend ourselves in mind, body, and spirit can become the supreme motivation in life, and the source of greatest joy and usefulness.

❧

Worthwhile Quest

LICE FREEMAN PALMER, once president of Wellesley College, spent some time in her youth teaching a Sunday School class made up of young girls recruited from a city slum.

One Sunday, the idea came to her to ask the children, who were tragically dirty and unpromising, to find something beautiful in their homes, and to tell the other children about it the next Sunday. When the next Sunday came, one little girl who lived in a particularly dirty tenement said slowly, "I ain't found nothing beautiful where I live except the sunshine on our baby's curls."

Years later, long after Palmer's death, her husband was lecturing at a Western university and was entertained in a distinguished home. His hostess told him eagerly that she had once been a member of his late wife's Sunday School class.

"I can remember that your wife once asked us to find something beautiful in our homes," she said, "and that I came back saying the only thing I could find was the sunshine on my sister's curls. But your wife's suggestion was the turning point in my life. I began to look for something beautiful wherever I was, and I've been doing it ever since. It also encouraged me to look for something beautiful in everyone I meet and such a habit has enabled me to see the good I might have missed."

Each one of us is a walking bundle of habits. It is a plus when one of the habits is the practice of seeing the good and commenting on it. Such a habit means that the viewer, although not blind to the aspects of life, does not choose to always make them the focus.

There are times when legitimate complaints are in order. To pretend that something is good when it is not is a violation of integrity and may delay the remedy of an ill that needs correction. But imperfection is only one aspect of every human life. It takes no great skill to discover another's frailties. ("A preacher's faults," said Luther, "are soon spied.")

Conscientious people know that the central question to be addressed is, "How do we express love, and how can we best help another?" It is not in concentrating on others' weaknesses. Doing so accentuates the imperfection, both in the mind of the viewer and of the one who is criticized.

Jesus was not unaware of the weaknesses of his disciples, but he appealed to their strengths and turned even potential liabilities into assets. The pugnacity of Peter could have been an occasion for criticism, but Jesus saw it as a virtue, and harnessed Peter's fiery energies to worthy ends.

Great teachers have always encouraged others to love and to look for the good. Love is not blind. It is the only reality that sees. It calls into being those things that are hidden from human eyes, but nonetheless real. Love awakens sleeping beauty. It encourages the best.

"Dig deep enough into any human being," said Saint Augustine, "and you will find something divine."

Marriages are happier in homes where the compliments outnumber the complaints. There is no merit in looking for the worm in the apple of your eye. The grave of love is dug with little digs.

Wise parents emphasize encouragement rather than censure. Praise is to the child what sunshine and rain are to the flower. We tend to become what others believe we are.

A friend tells of noticing a woman and her four children on the train a few years ago. She didn't try to interest the children in the scenery, a story, or a game, but only sought to restrain them. Her conversation was a mere series of, "No... Stop... Don't do that." When one little fellow ran to the end of the car beyond the range of vision, she sent the older sister after him, saying, "Go see what Will is doing and tell him to stop it."

She seemed to assume that everything they did was wrong, and in the atmosphere she created, the assumption was pretty nearly correct.

There are those who have the curious impression that to praise a person is to make that person conceited. Almost without exception, the reverse is the case. Appreciation induces humility. Few things are as humbling as warm-hearted recognition and approval. The recipient feels unworthy of what is said and wishes to make it true.

The minor tragedy of many lives is that people go on and on, week in and week out, never hearing a word of praise for their efforts from anyone. An office worker commented wistfully, "The only time my boss notices what I do is when I don't do it."

Thinking of the vast follies in human history and in life around us today, it is easy to be critical of human nature and human beings much of the time. But remembering the people we know who, with little money or education, and often poor health, put up a brave front to meet the day's work with serenity, makes human nature seem sublime.

> *In men whom men condemn as ill*
> *I find so much of goodness still,*
> *In men whom men pronounce divine*
> *I find so much of sin and blot,*
> *I do not dare to draw a line*
> *Between the two, where God has not.*

—Joaquin Miller

Slaves of Habit

OME TIME AGO, while shopping in downtown Seattle, I made an unscheduled visit to a friend whose business office was nearby. The secretary ushered me into my friend's study, explaining that he would be with me in a few minutes. On the wall was a sign: "Don't be irritated by interruptions. They are your reason for being."

I had intended to apologize to my friend for intruding into his busy schedule without an appointment. But when he entered the room, I pointed to the sign and said, "It is easy to see why you are calm in the midst of so many pressures. You have a good motto to guide you."

"Dale," he responded, "you give me more credit for calmness than the facts warrant, but happily, I do try not to be disturbed by interruptions. I have made it a habit through the years to leave a stretch factor in my daily schedule. I start early and have tried not to so crowd my day with appointments that I have no time for the unexpected. I have not seen interruptions as an intrusion. So welcome to my office, and thanks for coming."

My friend was demonstrating one of the marks of a well-organized life. His life has an elastic quality. It is equipped with expansion points. Already containing many interests and commitments, his daily schedule is flexible enough to make room for the unexpected and unplanned.

We all have our own routines, our well-ordered or well-planned days. "Plan your work and work your plan," makes for efficiency. How little we would achieve without routine and schedule. But when we make routine and schedule a security blanket or allow ourselves to become slaves of habit, permitting no room for interruption, we may miss something of greater value.

Wise people know there are times when there is need to interrupt their routines to open the door for new experiences, or to attend to something more urgent than what was planned.

Roland Daab, who died in December of 1990, has entered the *Guinness Book of World Records* for his seventy years perfect attendance at Saint Paul's United Church of Christ in Columbia, Illinois. His faithfulness in Sunday School and in worship services became a community legend.

I have visited by phone with members of his church and they told of his kindliness, caring, and the many ways in which he expressed his faith in daily life. This is good, for there is always the risk that, in achieving such a record, attendance could become an end in itself and an occasion for inordinate pride.

Had I known Mr. Daab, I might have been inclined to ask him gently, "Was there never a Sunday morning when your own infectious cold might have dictated that you interrupt your routine and stay home? Was there never a Sunday morning when an ill family member or sick friend needed you to stand by? Was no day so incredibly beautiful as to lure you to the countryside or to the lake? Were there no interruptions of consequence to detour you, even for one Sunday?"

I might have asked these questions—not to downplay such a splendid record of loyalty or to encourage spasmodic church attendance (regularity in church attendance is a highly commendable habit), but I think even a routine that is solemnized because it is tied to the church may well blind us to a larger opportunity or greater responsibility.

"Man's interruptions are God's opportunities." This old proverb will hang on a prominent wall of any who desire to serve. When we have dedicated our lives to God's will, all moments offer opportunities for learning or helpfulness even though they might not have been planned.

On Palm Sunday, millions of Christians celebrate Jesus' triumphal entry into Jerusalem. Hundreds of people welcomed him into that ancient city centuries ago. Jesus was popular with the common people, for he spoke in a manner that enabled them to understand and feel a sense of worth. His was a busy life, but he was never too busy to be accessible to people of every class and age.

In the tenth chapter of Mark we read that the people brought children to Jesus to have him touch them, but the disciples reproved them and tried to protect

Jesus from interruption.

When Jesus saw what they were doing, he was indignant and said to them, "Let the children come to me; do not try to stop them, for the Kingdom of God belongs to such as they. I tell you, whoever does not accept the Kingdom of God like a child shall not enter it at all."

There are times when our unwillingness to welcome an interruption can deny us a larger experience or a meaningful friendship.

Some years ago, two young men were on a vacation in Scotland. Wandering in one of the great mountain glens as night began to fall, they realized they had lost their way. Seeing a light in the distance and guessing it came from some lonely cottage, they made their way there and asked for shelter. The occupants did not welcome interruption of their routine, and entertaining strangers was not in their plans, so they did not offer hospitality and the two brothers were turned away.

One of those young men became King George V of England. How the folks in that cottage must have lamented their inhospitality if they ever learned who they had turned away. But there is royalty in everyone we meet, for God dwells in all, and the way we treat people is the way we treat God.

Starting & Staying

T THE BEGINNING of each new year, we like to make resolutions about how we'd like to improve ourselves. It is easy to become excited about next year's program of reform. It is much more difficult to follow through when the new year is under way.

The qualities of life that lead us to launch an enterprise with zeal and enthusiasm may not be accompanied by the qualities that will enable us to see it through to a successful finish. Good starters and good stayers are not necessarily the same people.

A marathon runner was asked, "What is the hardest part of the long run—the first nine miles, the-middle nine miles or the last nine miles?" Without hesitation, the runner replied, "The middle nine miles." During the first nine miles, he was fresh and strong. When he reached the last nine miles, his spirit revived because the goal was in sight. "But it is during the middle nine miles I feel most like quitting," he said. "That's when the run loses its glamour and becomes a grind."

When we begin any new venture or try to break a

long standing bad habit, we discover the early hours are filled with the glow of high purpose. But then come the difficult daily demands that call for unswerving loyalty to the new task at hand.

How many dieters have started out excitedly on a rigorous program of restraint and have continued for a short time, only to succumb to the lure of certain high-caloried foods or a hunger pang or two?

How many have set for themselves a program of exercise, only to return to sedentary habits after a few sore muscles or an overpowering urge to watch TV?

How many have determined to pray, read Scriptures, and attend worship services loyally, only to give priority to staying in bed, reading the Sunday paper, playing golf, or going fishing?

Perhaps some measure of guilt we may feel for failed resolutions is traceable to the fact that we have set our immediate goal too high. Emerson's dictum, "Hitch your wagon to a star," has caused much frustration and feelings of guilt. It may be wiser to hitch your wagon to a higher plateau. When reaching that plateau, bask in the sense of accomplishment for a brief time. Then aspire to reach the next higher plateau. Continue on until you reach a mountaintop, and eventually, the moon or a star.

A different approach might be to have "New Day Resolutions" rather than New Year's Resolutions. Members of Alcoholics Anonymous set for themselves sobriety for one day. They achieve that. Then they accept the same goal for each succeeding day. They win their victory day by day.

Success is never automatic. Self-discipline and determination, and above all, persistence and perseverance are required. "Failure," goes an old proverb, "is the path of least persistence. By perseverance two snails reached the ark."

An ambitious young man approached a successful businessman with, "Please tell me the secret of your success." "There is no secret," was the reply. "You just jump at your opportunity."

"But how can I know when my opportunity comes?" The young man asked. "You can't," the businessman said. "You have to keep jumping."

On the other hand, the wayside of business is full of brilliant people who started out as jumpers and lacked the stamina to finish. Their places were taken by patient and unshowy plodders who never knew when to quit.

The late Ray Kroc, founder of the McDonald's food chain was such a person. "It is amazing," he said, "what one person of average skill can accomplish if he has constancy of purpose and the willingness to 'keep on keeping on.'"

In keeping on, McDonald's has provided employment for more young people in America than any other commercial venture. It was from President Calvin Coolidge that Kroc borrowed the motto entitled, "Press On." Scrolled and framed, it bedecks the tiled kitchens of McDonald's franchises across the world:

Nothing in the world can take the place of persistence.

Talent will not: nothing is more common than

unsuccessful men of talent.

Genius will not: unrewarded genius is almost a proverb.

Education will not: the world is full of educated derelicts.

Persistence and Determination alone are omnipotent.

Are we determined to invigorate or renew our resolutions each day? Right now is a good time to begin.

Thank God It's Today

THE HECTIC PACE of daily life brings many ills. One of them is debilitating fatigue. Some measure of tiredness is normal. It makes bedtime a delight. But inordinate fatigue works against the joy of living and makes us less effective in our work.

One man confessed, "I recognize that it takes a lot of integrity to know whether I'm really tired or just lazy, but often, when it's only Tuesday, I'm exhausted all the way to Friday. At work, I'm usually done before the day is."

Fatigue affects not only our work but our worship as well. Sometimes, the trouble with Sunday morning is Saturday night. There are those who arrive at church unprepared for worship. An exhausting week and a late Saturday night have so depleted the body of its receptive powers that even the most eloquent preacher would have difficulty making the theme of the morning interesting to them.

Such a worshiper was led down the aisle by an usher who asked, "How far down do you want to sit?" "All the way, my friend, all the way," said the weary worshiper.

In the book, *Fatigue in Modern Society*, edited by Paul Tournier, we are told that fatigue comes not so much from hard work as from rebellious and unresolved conflicts within ourselves.

These are harder to deal with.

Doctors tell us that patients generally submit voluntarily to prescriptions for medicines or rest cures for fatigue, but that they are reluctant to change their way of living. Patients hope there is something they can take that will assure their healing without their having to give up whatever compromised their health and vigor in the first place.

It is not enough to prescribe tonics, vitamins, tranquilizers, sedatives, pep pills, or other drugs, even though it is incontestable that the overuse of drugs in our society is in an effort to maintain vitality. This proves that there are better ways to guard against excessive fatigue and assure stamina for each day's living.

Wise people are selective in choosing what they do and do not do. They learn to say "no" to unimportant or unnecessary requests. Conscientious or achievement-oriented people are the most vulnerable. The desire to be helpful and to be involved is commendable, but it carries with it the risk of over-commitment and exhaustion.

"If you are between fifty and seventy," said T.S. Eliot, "you are the most vulnerable, for you are always being asked to do things, and you are not decrepit enough to turn them down." Some of us schedule our lives too full. We have built an altar to energy and made activity our god. Like Stephen Leacock's famous rider, we get on our horse and ride off in all directions.

Many business and professional women and men who would not think of putting too much pressure in their automobile tires are constantly putting more pressure on the heart and arteries than is wise. They "catch" a bus, "grab" a bite to eat, "contact" a client, and are continually on the go. They also often fall asleep at the wheels of their automobiles.

Good distance runners learn to pace themselves. They learn to let go to be able to hang on—to read the handwriting on the wall before they have to read it on the ceiling. An epitaph in a New England cemetery reads:

> *Here lies extinguished in his prime*
> *A victim of modernity,*
> *Just yesterday, he hadn't time*
> *And now he has eternity.*

Happy are those who learn how to delegate responsibility. Mothers and dads who do all the household chores themselves not only wear themselves out, but deny other members of the household meaningful participation and a chance to learn. All successful leaders know how to assign responsibility to others.

In Exodus 18:13-37, we read that Moses was carrying the full load of administrative detail for the Hebrew Exodus from Egypt. He made all the decisions, and it was killing him by degrees. I wouldn't be surprised if Zipporah, his wife, didn't whisper in her father's ear a plea encouraging him to tell Moses to cool it.

"He's trying to do it all alone," she may have said. "He won't listen to me, but he might listen to you."

In any case, we do know that Moses' father-in-law, Jethro, did say to Moses, in effect, "It is no mystery why you are tired and becoming less effective. You can't do all this alone."

Heeding the advice of Jethro, Moses appointed deputies so that the work was done and the Hebrews were soon again on their way.

God does not judge us by the multitude of works we perform, but by how well we do the work that is ours to do. The happiness of too many days is often destroyed by trying to accomplish too much in one day. We would do well to follow a common rule for our daily lives: *Do less and do it better.*

BEING

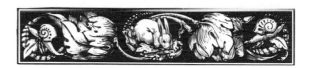

Self-Respect

SYCHOLOGISTS TELL US that if you ask the average person to list his personality strengths, he will come up with only five or six. But, asked to do the same for his weaknesses, the list will be two or three times as long.

It is intelligent to have a fair assessment of our skills and personality traits, and not to think too highly of ourselves. But it is intelligent, too, to appreciate the positive qualities that are ours. Think long enough about our limitations and they will be ours. Center on the pluses, and they will grow.

A self-employed man in England named A. Hancock gave evidence that he appreciated himself and the contribution he had made to life through his work. At the hour of his retirement, he bought a watch and had it inscribed: "Presented to myself by myself in recognition of fifty-five years work I have done while working for myself. Thanking me, I am A. Hancock. 1849-1904." The attainment of proper self-love and respect is one of life's highest attainments.

When people are enslaved by wrong attitudes

toward themselves, they cannot help but express wrong attitudes toward others. We give to others not only what we have, but what we are. All living with others begins with self.

"Thou shalt love the Lord thy God with all thy heart, and with all thy soul, and with all thy strength, and with all thy mind, and thy neighbor as thyself." Perhaps in teaching this greatest commandment in our churches, we have stressed the aspect of loving our neighbor to the neglect of loving ourselves.

Jesus did not say to hate ourselves, but to love others in the same proportion that we love ourselves. If some loved others only to the degree they love themselves, there would be little love to give to others.

Too often the teaching of the church in sermon and song has encouraged people to think less highly of themselves than they ought. An old hymn, sung years ago, was titled, "O to Be Nothing, Nothing." In a world that desperately needed something, they were praying in song to be ciphers—nonentities.

We are not writing about the kind of self-love that sets self above others. That is pride in the negative sense. There are those who have an exaggerated sense of their own importance. They are like the rooster that thought the sun rose every morning just to hear him crow.

Those who have read my writings know that I do not avoid involvement in social issues, for I believe that people who profess religion have a responsibility to the whole of society. But good religion does not deal simply with society as a whole. It deals with the individual as well. A religion that ends with self is no worthy religion at all, but a religion that doesn't begin with self is equally inadequate and distorted.

Only when we start appreciating the high value of something are we likely to deplore its prostitution. It is said that a servant once beat a rug with his master's flute. The servant was content with the performance, but the owner was not, for he knew what a flute was for. He raged at its misuse. So great religion, loftily estimating what human personality was meant to be, has raged against that which would abuse it.

There would be less violence, alcoholism, drug addiction, and promiscuity if there were more who had a finer sense of their own inner sanctities. The best parents, teachers, and preachers do not so much thunder against sin as they heighten the listener's conception of life's dignity and supreme worth.

In Arthur Miller's play, *Death of a Salesman,* Willie Loman, the main character, is a lovable person in many ways, but he desecrates everything fine and good. He didn't love himself enough to avoid being caught up in practices which profaned his personality and destroyed what was sacred and holy within him. At his grave a comment was made by one of the mourners before his body was laid to rest: "Poor Willie, he didn't know who he was."

There is much nonsense today in talking about the sins of society, as though society were a kind of organism or personality that could be, of itself, moral or immoral, apart from the people who constitute it. Good or evil, prejudice or love, are first of all inside individuals and only secondarily in their relations.

There are many who are worried about the future of our nation. The proliferation of violence, drugs, racism, and homicides frightens any sensitive person. Our hope lies in proportion to the number of young people, men and women, who have such intense love for, and pride in, themselves that they will permit no room for bigotry, hatred, or prejudice.

Our country will be only as great as the individuals who make up its citizenry. Government, organization, and structure are important, but it is the quality of the fabric which determines the real strength of our nation.

Gift of Humility

LMOST ANYONE WOULD acknowledge that humility is necessary if life is to be gracious and beautiful. Yet, as a whole, we do not give top priority to it. Other virtues—self-cultivation, self-realization, self-expression—we have specialized in, but not humility.

Our generation is not the first to give lesser consideration to humility. Highly intelligent people have bypassed it when setting goals for their lives.

Benjamin Franklin made a list of twelve virtues he wanted to incorporate in his life. Each week he concentrated on one of these virtues and then moved on to the next. After the twelve-week cycle was completed, he began again to concentrate on the first. With this kind of strategy he hoped, over a period of years, to build into his life a habit pattern wherein all these virtues would find natural expression.

He showed his list to a friend who was quick to point out that he omitted the most important virtue of all—humility. Franklin recognized this and quickly added it to his list.

Franklin placed humility last on his list of virtue, but Jesus put it first in his Beatitudes: "Blessed are the poor in spirit (the humble) for theirs is the Kingdom of Heaven."

Humility is not simply an added grace that makes other virtues more presentable and likable. Humility is the foundation for all other virtues. Humility is teachability. It is eagerness to learn and grow.

Modesty is not self-disparagement, but rather appraising ourselves at our true value. The derivation of the word modest is instructive. It comes from the Latin, and is derived from modus, a measure, and so comes to mean the measuring facility.

Modesty, therefore, means not underestimating ourselves, but correctly estimating ourselves. It avoids self-disparagement on the one hand, and on the other it prevents us from thinking more highly of ourselves than we ought to think.

Self-esteem and self-conceit are opposites. It is not conceit to take pride in ourselves, our family, our work, our country, and all that is worthy of our best.

An unlettered scrubwoman employee of a bank, who, in telling her neighbor of her work, spoke with unconcealed but defensible pride: "When I begun scrubbing and polishing those floors at the bank they was in bad shape, but since I've been doing them, three ladies has fell down!" We rejoice in her workmanship and her delight in doing a thorough job!

There are, however, those who, in singing their own praises, get the pitch too high. "One of my chief regrets during my years in the theater," said John Barrymore, "is that I couldn't sit in the audience and watch me."

When an attorney, during a trial, characterized Frank Lloyd Wright as America's greatest architect, Wright confessed to his wife that he couldn't deny it, for he was under oath.

It is possible to be guilty of group pride. A Carthusian monk, explaining to an inquirer the distinctive feature of his order, said, "When it comes to good works we are no match for the Benedictines: as to preaching, we are not in the same class with the Dominicans: the Jesuits are way ahead of us in scholarship and learning: but when it comes to humility—we are tops!"

Humility can be illustrated more easily than it can be defined.

Humility is Sir Isaac Newton, saying, "I do not know what I may appear to the world, but to myself I seem to have been only like a boy playing on the seashore, and in diverting myself in now and then finding a prettier shell, or smoother pebble than ordinary, whilst the great ocean of truth lay all undiscovered before me."

Humility is Robert Louis Stevenson, after struggling for a lifetime against what seemed insurmountable troubles, yet producing immortal words to enrich the world, he penned his own epitaph: "Here lies one who meant well, tried a little, and failed much."

Humility is the college football lineman writing home to his father on Saturday evening: "Dear Dad— We lost today, six to nothing. The other team found a big hole in the center of our line, and that big hole was me!"

Humility is Pope John XXIII saying, "Anybody can be Pope. The proof is that I have become one."

Humility is Mother Teresa saying: "I am just a little pencil in God's hand."

> *The dear Lord's best interpreters*
> *Are humble human souls;*
> *The Gospel of a life like theirs*
> *Means more than books or scrolls.*

❧

Being Rich

 FEW YEARS AGO there died in Paris a woman who had the dubious reputation of being the best dressed woman in Europe. After her death it was found that the chief item of her legacy to the world was a wardrobe containing almost a thousand frocks. She was practically smothered in a closet of clothes. Garments became the limit of her horizon.

Think how having a thousand possible changes of costume would complicate life! Imagine the strain of having to decide every morning which one of a thousand costumes we would wear for the first hour of the day. That is a burden from which God in his mercy has relieved most of us.

Yet no one is immune to the possibility of a similar fate. We are never free from the insistent persuasion to buy and earn ever more. Enough is never quite enough. The modern hero is the poor boy who becomes rich rather than the Franciscan or Buddhist ideal of the rich boy who voluntarily becomes poor.

We are made to feel ashamed to wear clothes or drive cars until they are worn out. The mass media have convinced us that we are out of step with reality. It is time to awaken to the fact that conformity to a sick society is sick. We must take exception to the modern psychosis that defines people by how much they can acquire or what they can earn.

Until we see how unbalanced our culture has become, we will not be able to deal with the mammon spirit of acquisitiveness that destroys our inner peace, satisfaction, and appreciation for what we do have.

Ambition is to be lauded. The willingness to work hard to increase skills in order to earn more is a commendable trait. We have need for enough money to meet our bills and to enjoy some of the amenities that bring quality to our lives. Life is a matter of balance. "It is preoccupation with possession," said Bertrand Russell, "more than anything else that prevents us from living freely and nobly."

We are slow in learning the lessons the wise would teach us. Jesus said, "A man's life consists not in the abundance of things he possesses."

"A man is rich," said Thoreau, "in proportion to the things he can afford to leave alone."

John Stuart Mill, the brilliant English philosopher and economist, said, "I have learned to seek my happiness by limiting my desires rather than attempting to satisfy them."

Many years ago, Rudyard Kipling delivered a commencement address at McGill University in Montreal. He said one striking thing that deserves to be remembered. He was warning the students, against an overconcern for money, position, or glory. He said:

"Someday you will meet a man who cares for none of these things. Then you will know how poor you are."

There are individuals who have revealed to us where life's real values reside. One of them died in London in 1912. Unlike the woman in Paris, he had only one frock in his wardrobe.

I have seen a dozen pictures of him, always in that same suit. It was a blue suit, with a red collar on the coat. The man who wore it was William Booth, founder of the Salvation Army.

Just one costume, but a man with a thousand lives. He took on himself the loads that rested on a thousand backs and felt keenly the sharp edges of life that cut into others. He wrapped the cloak of compassion around broken men and women and left a legacy of thousands of changed lives.

Halford Luccock, one of Yale Divinity School's finest teachers, pointed out that the two most notable figures in the history of Africa in the nineteenth century were Cecil Rhodes and David Livingstone.

Rhodes amassed millions exploiting South Africa, with its gold and its diamonds. His desire to seize all of South Africa for the British Empire was one of the chief causes of the Boer War. Rhodes died worth many millions of dollars.

The other figure was a missionary and explorer, Livingstone. He gave his life not only to bring the gospel of Jesus to the black people of Central Africa, but also to fight against slavery and all the oppressions that beset them. He died with hardly a cent to his name. But his grave in Westminster Abbey is one of the greatest shrines of the world.

When we look at Livingstone, who cared for none of these prizes that make life a fitful fever for so many, we see how poor Cecil Rhodes really was.

∽

True Beauty

VERY YEAR, A certain magazine carries the names and pictures of ten of the nation's "most beautiful people." This term—*beautiful people*—has long confused me because most of the time I am not sure what it means. I have noticed that the reference is usually to jet-setters in high society, the chic people whose photographs populate the glossies—stunningly handsome professional models and ravishingly good-looking men and women. I take it these are the "beautiful people."

Perhaps to be physically endowed in such a way as to gain favorable glances from others could be a source of personal satisfaction, and I have no desire to be churlish about it. But it strikes me that we often use the word "beautiful" carelessly. I believe that in our everyday lives we are surrounded by people who are truly beautiful and yet we may not be aware of it. Their beauty is not publicized and pictured, but it is very real.

Years ago I was introduced to a woman who was short and plump—nearly as wide as she was tall—with no redeeming facial features. Surely, I thought, here is one of the most unattractive people I have ever met. There we stood, face to face—two people with the same thought at the same time!

However, as time passed and our friendship deepened, I came to regard her as one of the most beautiful persons I knew. Her eyes were deep with eternal wisdom, and her kindness and caring endeared her to all who knew her. To see her walking down the street was to wonder what particular mission of helpfulness she was then engaged in.

Elizabeth Barrett Browning described such a woman in her lovely poem, "My Kate." The first two of seven verses I include here:

> She was not as pretty as women I know,
> And yet all our best made of sunshine and snow
> Drop to shade, melt to naught in the long-trodden
> ways,
> While she's still remembered on warm and cold days—
> My Kate.

> Her air had a meaning, her movements a grace;
> You turned from the fairest to gaze on her face;
> And when you had once seen her forehead and mouth
> You saw as distinctly, her soul and her truth—
> My Kate.

I suspect that what I am saying is best summarized in what many of us heard from parents, grandparents, and teachers when we were young, "Beauty is as beauty does."

The truly beautiful people are those whose lives witness to a strength of character and are, therefore, spiritually beautiful—an aged woman of indomitable spirit who barely survives on a Social Security check and moves in our midst with great dignity; a man whose every step is an act of courage because of painful arthritis; a father and mother who have lost a child to drug traffickers, and who work, love, hope and pray daily for his release from the prison of addiction; a person who struggles with faith and good cheer in the presence of a disease that depletes energy and affords little relief from discomfort; a single parent who works outside the home, provides day care for her children, returns home, cooks, irons, and reads to youngsters before dropping wearily into bed.

Those who meet all the wrinkles of advancing years with acceptance and good spirit and are concerned that their lives reflect a beauty deeper than physical charm— these are the truly beautiful people. They radiate a spiritual loveliness that refuses to be dimmed. Without knowing it, they strengthen us and make the whole world more beautiful because they dwell within it.

Smiles of Access

VERY SO OFTEN, out of the thousands of words that rain down upon us day after day, one word gets through and sticks. It captures the attention, and sends the imagination soaring. Some time ago, the word *approach* struck me in this way—*approach* and its cognates *approachable* and *approachability* and the negative, *unapproachable*.

In a world such as ours—a world of bridges and tunnels, huge buildings and super highways—approaches are critically important.

Functionally, of course, there must be a way of getting to the bridge or into the building, or off the freeway into a particular community or section of the city. I sometimes think that speed reading should be required in our schools to prepare us for getting off the freeway at the right time.

The proliferation of freeways and the need for access and egress has led us to think of a cloverleaf as something gray and made of concrete, rather than something green that grows in the ground.

Approaches are more than functional. They have a

psychological character as well. They prepare us for an experience. If, in approaching a restaurant, you find a canopy out front and a doorman standing watch, you expect good food, but you had better be prepared for high prices.

Approaches have a way of conditioning our expectations. They hint at what is coming.

The doorman, if asked, is likely to tell us that if we have to inquire about the prices, we might be well-advised to stay away.

Approaches can create images. In a day gone by, banks were known for their massive pillars and heavy doors overlaid with gleaming brass. The impression conveyed was one of safety. Today, the emphasis is on warmth and cordiality. Bank exteriors are not nearly so imposing. More glass is used. The image of the "friendly banker" begins with the approach. The accent now is not on security, but on trust and amiability.

> *(However, there is still one thing*
> *That puzzles thoughtful men,*
> *The bank trusts every customer*
> *But chains each ball point pen!)*

There are times when a receptionist betrays his or her reason for being—to receive—by giving the impression that you are an intruder, trespassing on time allocated for other matters. How refreshing to be greeted with a friendly smile and "Good morning! What goes well with you today?"

One of Jesus' most endearing and admirable traits

was his approachability. He was easily accessible to people who wanted to see him.

At times, of course, Jesus did retreat, but only to enlarge and deepen the self that he would make available to others.

In the Apostle Paul's letter to the Romans (12:13), he encourages Christians to practice hospitality. William Tyndale, in the sixteenth century, gave a graphic translation of hospitality. "Be ye," he said, "of an harborous disposition." That is, welcome others into your life in a cordial and loving way.

Our approachability is a matter of temperament. Our compassion, caring, and genuine friendliness is revealed in the way we receive others.

Individuals embossed with an undue sense of self-importance bear signs saying, "Keep out," "Do not enter," or "Enter at your own risk." Powerful waves of unfettered ego emanate from their presence, making approachability and warm relationships improbable.

Others who are unapproachable are those preoccupied with their own goals. Their rejections are subtle. They are highly selective as to what or who will be admitted to their harbor. Anyone who can do them good will get in. The "right" phone calls will get through. The "right" conferences will be set up.

Today, we may not have people knocking on our door for shelter, but in the course of our day, there are people (if we have eyes to see and insights to know) who are begging us to let them in out of a rough and troubling sea.

"Be ye of an harborous disposition."

One of the most moving experiences in the White House happened during President Eisenhower's administration. A young girl who had been blind since birth was brought to meet Mamie Eisenhower to start a national fund drive. The first lady was never enthusiastic about public appearances, but this was a good cause. When Mrs. Eisenhower appeared, the blind girl's mother explained to her daughter that the president's wife was approaching. "Oh Momma," asked the excited youngster, "am I smiling?"

Are you approachable? Are you smiling?

~

Enthusiasm

ANY OF US are equipped with efficient self-starters. We get under way early. We are off with fleet eagerness, but our interest wanes and our best intentions go unrealized.

It is important to cultivate what the New Testament calls "patient continuance."

The life that achieves anything requires enthusiasm and staying power. These are attributes rarely celebrated by poets but they have a great deal to do with the history of the species. Every worthwhile achievement since the beginning of the world has been the result of someone's enthusiasm and a willingness to persevere. Helen Keller said, "We can do anything we want if we stick to it long enough."

Enthusiasm is the key word. It helps keep staying power alive. Some have enthusiasm for thirty minutes—others have it for thirty days. But is is those who have it for thirty years who make the maximum contribution to life.

Without enthusiasm, no battles have been won, no *Iliad*s written, no empires founded, no religions propagated. The secret of success in any endeavor is enthusiasm. The people of victory are those who have kept the fires burning on the altars of enthusiasm when other flames have died.

Enthusiasm can make even a monotonous job interesting. Without it we plod drearily through a task that might often be a real adventure. We must all submit to a certain amount of sheer drudgery or routing, and have to perform many tasks that are not especially enjoyable. A friend of mine uses the phrase, "dumb things we have to do."

William Lyon Phelps, who was one of Yale's greatest professors, asked William R. Harper, one-time president of the University of Chicago, at the end of a long lecture day, "How do you keep so enthusiastic so late in the day, especially after teaching a subject as dry as Hebrew?"

"Well," Dr. Harper replied, "if I have no enthusiasm, then I create it."

Howard Thurston (1869-1936), the great magician, knew the importance of psyching himself before each performance. He created the enthusiasm he needed by isolating himself before each show. In a room offstage, he paced back and forth, reminding himself of the importance of that particular performance.

He said to himself, "Hundreds of people have traveled many miles to see this show. They have spent their hard earned money and are giving their precious time to be here tonight. I must not disappoint them with a lackluster performance."

His isolation and self pep talk enabled him to create the enthusiasm he needed to be at his best.

I was impressed years ago when I read an article written by Halford Luccock in which he told that Eugene Ormandy dislocated his shoulder while leading the Philadelphia Symphony Orchestra. I do not know what they were playing. Probably not Mozart. Perhaps Stravisnksy. But at any rate, he was giving all of himself to it. And I have asked myself sadly, "Did I ever dislocate anything in my preaching—even a necktie?"

Certainly John Wesley did. He was asked how it was that so many came to hear him preach. Wesley replied, "I just set myself on fire and people come to watch me burn." He believed that if the heart was afire, some sparks would fly out of the mouth.

Lincoln said, "I like to see a man preach like he was fighting bees."

We like to see anyone tackle the work that is hers or his with enthusiasm. A sportswriter pointed out that Willie Mays played baseball with a boy's glee, a pro's sureness, and a champion's flair. He never lost his enthusiasm for the game. From the stands it always looked like he was having fun—and he was!

Often an athletic team, seemingly less qualified for a victory, defeats a team with more skilled players simply because they bring more enthusiasm to the contest. Sometimes reporters refer to that enthusiasm as *heart*. The actual derivation of the word from early Greek means "having a god within."

It is heartening to know that when we tackle the mundane tasks with enthusiasm, with energy, and with cheerfulness, we find a joy and fulfillment in doing them that we had not anticipated.

The words of Henry Van Dyke are worth thinking about as we meet each day's responsibilities:

> *Let me but do my work from day to day*
> *In field or forest, at the desk or loom,*
> *In roaring market place or tranquil room;*
> *Let me but find it in my heart to say,*
> *When vagrant wishes beckon me astray,*
> *"This is my work, my blessing not my doom,*
> *Of all who live, I am the one by whom*
> *This work can best be done in the right way."*
> *Then shall I see it not too great or small*
> *To suit my spirit and to prove my powers;*
> *Then shall I cheerful greet the laboring hours,*
> *And cheerful turn, when the long shadows fall*
> *At eventide, to play and love and rest.*
> *Because I know for me my work is best.*

∾

BELIEVING

Our Beliefs

HAT WE BELIEVE is of utmost importance. We live by believing something, not by debating and arguing about many things. Activity, to be effective, must spring from firmly held beliefs and convictions.

And well-ordered beliefs are a great asset, for they serve as an inner gyroscope giving stability and wise guidance in a world of turbulent transition.

When we think of the wide diversity of belief among thoughtful people, and the still wider diversity of temperament, education, and environment which helps to explain and perpetuate it, one can well be leery of formulating any statement of belief that would be generally acceptable to all. It's difficult to write, in a few hundred words, what we believe and why.

I feel uncomfortable and presumptuous in doing so, but there are certain beliefs that have guided my days, and I share them with the hope that some readers will find in what I have written either expressions of their own beliefs or stimulus to formulate their own.

I believe that human nature is neither intrinsically

good nor intrinsically evil, but individuals are born with different combinations of innate potentialities. They can be trained and nurtured to create, trust, love, and serve or to destroy, fear, and hate. I have seen enough of sordidness, selfishness, meanness, and brutality to be aware of human depravity. But I have also seen enough of kindness, generosity, nobility, and courage to prevent me from being cynical or pessimistic. I believe we have not begun to tap the limit of human potential for good. Democracy is based on the conviction that there are extraordinary powers in ordinary people.

I have faith in the human heart to grow toward the light. Despite daily headlines prophesying destruction, I believe we will build a world of peace and brotherhood. Peoples of our world have much more in common with one another than they have differences.

I am a long-range optimist. I like to view human progress in centuries rather than in years. I do not believe progress is automatic, nor does any optimism relieve me of a sense of urgency in working for human betterment.

I am not my brother's keeper, but I am called to be my brother's helper. I believe I have an obligation to work to create a social order in which people are more important than things, ideas more precious than gadgets, and in which individuals are judged on the basis of personal worth.

There are no unimportant people. Everyone is someone. Dig deep enough into anyone and we will find something divine.

I believe that to do unto others as we would have them do unto us is not simply a scriptural injunction or a law of duty, it is also a law of health that we violate at our own risk. Where we violate it we injure ourselves, inhibit our powers, blunt our sense of reality, limit our friendships, condemn ourselves to fear, guilt, and hostility, progressively isolate ourselves from others, and condemn ourselves to loneliness.

It is both good religion and common sense to be tender with the young, compassionate with the aged, sympathetic with the striving, tolerant with the weak and wrong, for sometime in life, we have been all of these.

I believe that whatever the purpose of life, it does not seem that we are to be carried to the skies on flowery beds of ease. Life will be easier if we begin with the recognition that it is hard. Discovering this reality is not an occasion for despair. Sorrow and adversity open doors to many of life's goods that respond to no other key. Nothing that can ever happen to us is half so important as the way we meet it.

God's resources are within grasp of all. The Creator's undergirding love enables us to sustain difficult days without being crushed or embittered by them.

I believe it is imperative not only to plan for the future but to savor the present. Each day brings twenty-four hours, not to pass but to fill. Frequently, I sit back and say to myself: let me make note of the moment I'm living right now, because in it I'm well, happy, hard at work doing what I enjoy, with family and friends I love. It won't always be like this. So while it is, I'll make the most of it, and afterward I'll remember and be grateful.

If we are alive and growing, it is to be hoped and expected that our beliefs will undergo change. Mohandas Gandhi often changed his mind publicly. An aide once asked him how he could so freely contradict this week what he had said just one week before. "Because," the great man replied, "this week I know better." Such openness and humility are goals worthy for all.

Heaven on Earth

HEN HENRY DAVID Thoreau was near death, his friend, Parker Pillsbury, leaned over his bed and whispered, "Do you have any vision of things beyond, David?" Thoreau responded, "One world at a time, Parker, one world at a time."

Jesus would have been in total agreement with Thoreau. Jesus said very little about heaven, but there is hardly a line in which he does not mention our earthly existence. What critics of the Christian religion never seem to understand is that the idea of a future life of some sort, which we commonly call heaven, is only a hope. It is not the central fact of the Christian faith.

The idea that Christians try to lead good lives only to be able to go to heaven is false. The idea that Christianity blinds the eyes of its followers and dulls their minds to the brutal facts of this world by presenting them with a lovely picture of the paradise awaiting them is not true. Those who sneer at Christianity because of its other-worldliness have really never understood it.

Far from being interested in some vague paradise

that was to come, Jesus was so concerned with this world that he believed and taught that heaven and eternal life were not simply in the future, but started here on earth. Jesus taught that anyone who was willing to accept his way of life on earth, and who lived that way abundantly, could here and now be in the presence of the eternal. This is the central fact of the Christian faith.

Heaven begins on earth for those who are unselfish and caring, who are sensitive to beauty both in nature and in human life, and who live with a consciousness of God's continuous presence.

Eternal life is not a postponed affair that comes after death. It is a way of living in this world which has nothing to do with death.

Easter has little to tell us about what we shall be in the next world, or what the next world is like. Easter's message is for now. It says that life in God is endless and unconquerable. This is the meaning of the Resurrection. It is the final proof of all Jesus had taught his disciples about eternal life.

So deathless was Christ's living that there was no stone heavy enough, no grave deep enough, no seal strong enough, no soldier powerful enough, to kill that kind of life.

When Jesus told the disciples, "I go to prepare a place for you," he did not describe the dimension or the nature of that place, and when he appeared before his disciples after the Resurrection, it was not to tell them of a beautiful heaven which was prepared to receive them sometime in the future. It was to show them that his way of life was deathless, that God's causes are never lost causes, and that there is a kind of life that is endless on earth and beyond the grave.

The disciples, who for a few days before his appearing had been grief-stricken by their loss, suddenly understood that their master's way of life was victorious even over death. They believed anew what they had heard him say: "I am the resurrection, and the life: he that believeth in me, though he were dead, yet shall he live, and whosoever liveth and believeth in me shall never die."

∽

Openness to All

NE OF THE sad aspects of life is that, in its brevity and limited energy, there is so much that is good that we never come to know—wonderful people we never meet, beautiful places we never see, inspiring and informative books we never read, great ideas we never entertain, and most regretful of all, marvelous religions and expressions of faith of which we know little or nothing.

In devotion to our faith and in loyalty to our own church or synagogue, we miss so much that is good that is being said and done in other religious bodies, even in our own community.

I have often wished that we could be cloned so that we could experience the helpful sermons being preached across the city in churches and synagogues other than our own. We would be lifted in spirit, too, by the friendship and good will of people of many faiths who are endeavoring to serve God's will in helpful ways.

Such an interchange would be most helpful, for it is amazing what areas of ignorance lie within the minds of seemingly cultivated people. Goodwill forums of Roman

Catholics, Protestants, and Jews have become popular. And yet in these groups which pride themselves on their culture and tolerance, it is frequently confessed that what each knows about other faiths is derived from writers of his own sect and all too often from anonymous documents at that.

Until we are willing to seek information from the other side of our social and religious fences, we cannot begin to lay claim to open-mindedness.

It is unfortunate that we do not study other major world religions as we study our own. Such a discipline of learning would eliminate many misconceptions and enable us to see the commonalities that bind us all.

My knowledge of religions other than Christianity is all too limited and sketchy, but I have in the study that I have done been able to see that each religion has its weaknesses and strengths and no one religion has full claim to the truth.

Arnold Toynbee said, "There is none alive today who knows enough to say with confidence whether one religion has been greater than all others."

In the limitation of space, I give only a glimpse of several of the great religions and encourage all to read Heston Smith's *The Religions of Man*.

The Jewish Talmud is the reservoir from which all of Judaism, Christianity, and Islam drew their basic moral code, many of their articles of faith, and the fundamentals of their theology.

The beginning and ending of the Torah are performing acts of living kindness and unselfishness. Is there a more beautiful and challenging statement in any religion than that found in Micah 6:8?

He has told you, O mortal, what is good;
And what does the Lord require of you
but to do justice, and to love kindness,
and to walk humbly with your God?

Ayatollah Khomeini prejudiced the minds of millions in their understanding of Islam by inciting violence and revenge beyond his religion's teachings. It is unfair to characterize anything by its worst expressions.

No religion has succeeded any better than Islam in inducing its members to feel the immediate presence of the deity, and none have equaled it in causing its adherents to be daily and almost hourly aware of their relation to Allah.

Islam was in some ways the earliest religion to oppose social discrimination and the subjection of women. The trouble is that Islam is as bad as other Western religions in rather aggressively assigning itself a kind of special relation to God, a kind of preferred position. Such a claim has no defense.

I have long pondered the words of Buddha and found in them much wise counsel:

Believe nothing because a so-called wise man said it.
Believe nothing because the belief is generally held.
Believe nothing because it was written in an ancient
    book.
Believe nothing because it was said to be of divine
    origin,

Believe nothing because someone else believes it.
Believe only what you yourself judge to be true.

A noble religious insight is that of bodhisattva, the Buddhist, who has at last achieved the right to enter nirvana, but who refuses the bliss until he has turned back and helped every other struggling person reach nirvana, which can of course be an indefinite postponement. This selfless concern stands in judgment of any religion that places personal salvation ahead of concern for all.

Many Christians find the essence of their faith expressed in the Sermon on the Mount in Matthew 5, 6, and 7, First Corinthians 13, and Romans 12. The New Testament's teachings come to focus in the words of Jesus, "By this will all know that you are my disciples, that you love one another."

The call, then, is not to less loyalty to our own faith, but openness to all—a willingness to listen and learn from others. It is not to point the finger of judgment but to extend the hand of friendship and the arm of love. When we draw closer to one another, we draw closer to the God who created us all.

A Stunning Riddle

ASTER SUNDAY WILL find the churches filled to overflowing. The cynic thinks he has the explanation. The Easter Festival is a fashion parade. It is like a national holiday, celebrated in conformity with long-established custom, stirring up agreeable associations in the mind, but otherwise making hardly any impression profound or lasting.

So the cynic argues. There is truth in what he says, but it is not the whole truth. We respond to Easter's call because there is a deep, inarticulate longing within each one of us to discover answers to the puzzling questions relating to death: If a man dies shall he live again? Does the human spirit so precariously and briefly housed in the physical body survive death when the body ceases to be? Is death another experience in life or is it finality? Is the only immortality we can know in the minds of those who remember us?

There are profound and perplexing questions and no glib or dogmatic answers will suffice. We who know so little of life cannot be expected to have all of the answers relating to death. The questions have added significance for all who have lost family members or friends. They cry out with Tennyson's Maud:

Ah, Christ, that it were possible
For one short hour to see
The souls we loved, that they might tell us
What and where they be.
But only silence from the grave and
We are left to believe as we will
As to their destiny.

The finest people differ in their beliefs concerning the hereafter. Some find it easy to believe in continuation of life beyond the grave. Others, equally devoted, take the road of reverent agnosticism. Some say they have no belief in or wish for a life after death. A grave marker covers the resting place of one who lived with such a philosophy:

Don't bother me now
Don't bother me never
I want to be dead
Forever and ever.

That was not the philosophy of Sir Wilfred Grenfell. He said, "I am very much in love with life. I want all I can get of it. I want more of it, after the incident of death, if there is any to be had."

Those of us who share Grenfell's love of life and hope for continuation beyond the grave recognize that we cannot prove its reality but we are forever trying to prove it because we believe in it. Our belief in life after death rests on moral faith in three fundamental affirmations:

- The supreme worth of each individual;
- The rationality of the universe and the integrity of God;
- The resurrection of Jesus.

Man is a strange creature, somewhat larger than an ape, much less clear of eye, more dull of ear than some beasts, somewhat less strong than an ox, a moderately-sized, mediocrely-equipped animal. He is only nine meals removed from savagery. Deny him food for three days and he will lie, cheat, and steal. And yet he is a reasoning and loving creature, capable of rising to great heights of nobility and self-sacrifice.

Human personality, no matter how commonplace or limited is of incalculable worth. We are made in the image of God. Is the human spirit, then, destined to glisten on the horizon as a soap bubble only to be disintegrated? Is life but a brief candle, gone when snuffed out? Not so! "What is excellent as God lives," said Emerson, "is permanent."

Some believe in an immortality of influence. We live on, they reason, in the minds of those who remember us, in our children, in their children and in the institutions we support. An immortality of remembrance is good, but it is not enough. The time will come when those who remember us will also be gone and institutions will cease to be. Scientists tell us that one day not even the ashes will remain of the planet we inhabit.

If Jesus, Socrates, Plato, Moses, Lincoln, and Gandhi are extinct, then the rationality of the universe can be questioned. To believe in immortality or endless life is the supreme act of faith in the reasonableness of God's work. Those who die prematurely, those who suffer a lifetime of crippling illnesses or know agonizing privations need more life beyond the grave to vindicate the justice of God. Ryan White, a victim of AIDS at eighteen, and little boys and girls whose sun goes down while it is yet day deserve opportunity for life and fulfillment such as most of us have known. The Christian faith affirms that the opportunity for realization of their potential will be present in the life beyond the grave. The manner of its fulfillment is unknown to us, but in its reality we deeply believe.

God has implanted deep within the human heart belief in eternal life. Has our creator perpetrated a great fraud upon us, permitting us to believe what can never be realized? Not so!

Tennyson says:

> *Thou wilt not leave us in the dust;*
> *Thou modest man, he knows not why,*
> *He thinks he was not made to die*
> *And thou hast made him:*
> *Thou art just.*

The validity of these affirmations is dramatically demonstrated in the Easter story. Death did not have the last word. God raised up Jesus from the dead and by his Resurrection vindicated the cause of righteousness, endorsed everything for which Jesus stood, demonstrated that the universe is on the side of goodness and truth. Jesus said, "Because I live you shall live also." In this we find hope and joy even in the presence of sorrow and death . Our loved ones continue in God's care, life has meaning and purpose, its ultimate end is not death but life eternal and God has given us not a dead leader, but a living Lord. "Lo, I am with you always."

Mystery of God

RE YOU FAMILIAR with the story of the little girl in art class who was busily at work, and when the teacher asked her what she was doing, she replied that she was drawing a picture of God? "But nobody knows what God looks like," responded the teacher. Confident, the little girl answered, "They will when I am through."

The little girl is not alone. We all paint our own mental pictures at least of what we conceive God to be. It has always been so. In the sixth century B.C., the Greek philosopher Xenophanes said that if oxen, lions, and horses could carve images, they would make God in their own image and likeness.

A Hindu student, after spending several years in America in study and travel, was asked his opinion of America. "I take it from what I hear and observe," he said, "that God is a Caucasian, an American, a Baptist and a Republican."

It is wise to recognize that we have, at best, only a partial understanding of God. We see through a glass darkly. We know in part. It requires eternity to know infinity. As Goethe said, "The highest cannot be spoken."

We must begin with a recognition of the mystery of God. We do a disservice to ourselves and to our faith by claiming certainties about God that we cannot fully know. It is really better to have no opinion than one that is unworthy. "An honest God is the noblest work of man," said Robert Ingersoll. And we must not let the partialness of our knowing discourage us in the quest.

In the middle of the eighteenth century, John Newton wrote "Amazing Grace," which has become one of the most popular hymns of the late twentieth century. Newton wrote the hymn when he came to realize that he had done nothing to earn the loving care bestowed by God. He was receiving life and eternal life as a gift through the grace—a surely amazing grace—of God.

"When I realized I was saved by God's grace," Newton said, "it was then that the shades began to go up and the light began to shine into my life. Then, my whole life became a quest for God."

Rather than being discouraged by the partialness of our knowledge of God, we can be encouraged by it. We are better off living in a world where our life is surrounded by mystery than to live in a world so small that our minds could fully comprehend it all. A God small enough for our total understanding would not be big enough to meet all the needs of all of us.

A healthy and reverent agnosticism is good because it encourages the questioning of accepted dogmas that are sometimes harmful in the attempt to forge a more solidly defensible faith. Sensitive persons are open to truth regardless of its origin or source. Such persons look to all disciplines of learning—archaeology, sociology, anthropology, psychology, and all other disciplines where truth can be found. The insights of the Bible have been helpful to those of us in the Jewish and Christian faith. It is not a consistent picture of God we see in the Scriptures. Early in the records we read of the Hebrew belief in polytheism, or many gods. The early Hebrew God was tribal, vengeful, God was anthropomorphic—possessing the features of a human. God walked in the garden in the cool of the day. He revealed his back, but not his face to Moses.

As the Hebrews became more enlightened, their conception of God was expanded. God became more humane, universal, and more loving of all until, in the fullness of time, God revealed himself most clearly in the person of Jesus. Again, a child gives a simple and direct description: "Jesus," said a little boy, "is the best picture God ever had taken."

The Bible affirms that God is Creator. Dr. Edwin Conklin, the eminent American biologist, said, "The probability of life originating by accident is comparable to the probability of the unabridged dictionary resulting from an explosion in a printing shop."

In the life and teachings of Jesus we learn what the Creator God is like. Jesus revealed that God is a god of love, a loving Creator who cares for his children. God is not a wicked despot. We never go beyond God's love no matter how great are our failings. There is no sin so small that God will condone it, but no sin so great that God will not forgive.

Jesus came to make God's love visible. Because we see God's love mirrored so clearly in the life of Jesus, we no longer need to cringe as slaves of holy fear seeking to appease the Creator's anger with sacrifice and self-inflicted pain. We may come to the Creator trustingly and unafraid.

Jesus taught that God's love is as international as the sun that shines on the just and the unjust. God's love knows no boundaries of race, class, or nationality. The Bible affirms that we are all children of God and that each life is sacred. There are no unimportant persons.

Jesus' estimate of human personality, its divine origin, spiritual nature, supreme worth, boundless possibility, and eternal destiny represents his most original contribution to human thought. This conception of humanity has left its impact heavily in Western Civilization with its emphasis on the sacredness and dignity of each individual. It has done more to influence Western democracy than any other one thing.

I became a minister years ago not because I had found God, but because I wanted to find God and to be in the company of people who were interested and earnest in their quest to find and know God. I have not been disappointed. Neophytes and beginners though we are, I am confident that when others ask us what each of us knows of God, we can respond as Dr. Daniel Poling responded: "Well, very little, but what I do know has changed my whole life."

❧

ACCEPTING

Alternate Routes

READER SENDS A letter pointing out that many Christians say there is no other way to God except through Jesus Christ. That belief troubles this reader because, to him, it seems to limit God's love and is unfair to many sensitive, kindly people of other faiths or of no faith at all.

Sometimes an isolated text becomes a theological stumbling block.

The belief questioned by our reader is based on what Peter wrote about Jesus in Acts 4:12: "Neither is there salvation in any other: for there is no name under heaven given among men whereby we must be saved."

For me, Jesus is my savior. If I follow him, he leads me toward God and a fuller realization of the being God created me to be. But can I be so dogmatic as to say that all who don't go this route are lost?

Of course not. The reader is correct. Such a conclusion is too exclusive and unfair.

Look at someone like Anwar Sadat. He was not a Christian. He was a Moslem. Four times each day he prayed to the God of his understanding. He risked his life for peace—indeed, he lost his life in the pursuit of peace. Can we believe that he has no eternal salvation simply because he was not committed overtly to Jesus?

No human has the wisdom or the prerogative to determine the destiny of another's soul. It is a great day in our lives when we realize that we are not the general manager of the universe.

The answer to salvation depends a lot on how we interpret the Scriptures and their purpose.

I remember sitting beside a young man on a plane trip from Los Angeles. He had his Bible in hand and read it throughout the flight. Frequently he interrupted his reading to share his interpretation with me. He too believed there is no salvation outside of commitment to Jesus.

Near the end of the trip, he closed the Bible, thumped his cover with his hand and said, "I belong to a Bible-believing church. Do you?"

"Yes," I said, "I do. But I don't think we interpret the Scriptures the same way as you do. We take the Bible seriously but not literally, which is not to say we do not believe in the Bible."

The man was obviously not convinced of my wisdom, so as we were leaving the plane, I shared a story with him:

Several years ago, five men sat around a pot-bellied stove in the cotton growing area of the Deep South in mid-winter. They were arguing as to which was the "right" religion and which offered the greatest assurance of salvation. It was a fruitless discussion because no one could agree.

Finally, they turned to an old fellow who had been sitting silently in the corner of the room puffing on his pipe. His wisdom was well known in that community and they invited him to arbitrate.

"You know, gentlemen," he said, "when the cotton is picked there are several ways to get it over the mountains to the gin. We can take the northern route—it is longer, but the road is better, and it often seems the wiser choice. Or we can take the southern route. It is shorter, but the road is filled with chuck holes and narrow bridges. Or we can go directly over the mountain, even though it's more perilous.

It is interesting, however, that when we reach the gin, the response of the man in charge is always the same. He doesn't ask which way we came. He simply asks, "Brother, how good is your cotton?"

I have not seen the young man since leaving the plane, but I pray for him, for we are all children of the same Father who "has the whole world in his hands," and in whose grace and mercy we all rest our lives.

Prejudices

AN INCIDENT RECORDED in the first chapter of the Book of John written in the first century mirrors a problem we are still facing:

Philip of Bethsaida had been called to be a disciple of Jesus. He started immediately to tell others of his newfound friend. He went to Nathaniel to share his enthusiasm for Jesus and to invite Nathaniel to become a disciple. "We have found him of whom Moses in the Law and the Prophets did write—Jesus of Nazareth, the son of Joseph."

Nathaniel was not impressed. He merely replied: "Nazareth? Can any good thing come out of Nazareth?"

Nathaniel obviously had a prejudice against all Nazarenes. No longer thinking of Nazareth's people as individuals deserving to be judged on their own merits, he lumped them together and rejected them all.

Nathaniel has long since been dead, but the sin of prejudice is still very much alive. It makes its home in the most prestigious places and resides with the most respectable men and women.

Nathaniel was a respectable person. When Jesus saw

him, he said: "Behold an Israelite in whom there is no guile." He was a respectable person all right, but the sin that lived with him was terrible.

Like Nathaniel, we are not born with prejudices. We acquire them. Fortunately, there are many who see how insidious prejudice can be. They guard their lives against it and encourage others to do the same.

There is for instance, a sensitive woman in a New Jersey suburb who tells of her eight-year-old daughter's first manifestation of religious prejudice. The little girl came home from school dropping the remark that she did not like a certain playmate. The mother, being an alert person, sensed that perhaps this was the beginning of a religious prejudice, for the disliked schoolmate had a Jewish name.

Figuring that she would nip prejudice in the bud, she told her daughter that the Jewish people had just as much to be proud of as any other people. "Don't you know," she said, "that Jesus was a Jew?"

The tiny girl thought for a moment then said, "Well, anyway, God was an American."

Such confused thinking is humorous and, in some measure, excusable in a child. But when prejudice persists in an adult it is sad, tragic, and even dangerous.

"The Jews," said Hitler. "Can any good come out of those people?" Judging all Jews as a group, he destroyed six million innocent people, denied them life, and took from the world the gifts they had to offer.

"Russia," many once said, "can any good come out of Russia?" Unable to distinguish between the people of the Soviet Union and the government under which they lived, some lumped them all together and rejected each one.

This was manifestly unfair. Sensible souls know that there are good Russian people and evil Russian people, just as there are good Americans and evil ones. People are people everywhere.

No more conspicuous illustration of the power of love in conquering prejudice could be cited than that of Lincoln's treatment of Edwin M. Stanton. During the presidential campaign, Stanton was reported to have spoken of Lincoln as, "a low, cunning clown, the original baboon."

Revenge might have seemed in order, but such a response had no place in the great emancipator's plans. He did not say, "Can any good come from Stanton?" Lincoln knew there were great possibilities in his life, so he appointed Stanton to his Cabinet.

A few years later, when the martyred leader lay dead, who stood by his bedside and said, "There lies the greatest ruler of men the world has ever seen"? It was Edwin M. Stanton, transformed by the power of love.

It was that same spirit of love that enabled Lincoln to begin breaking down the barriers of hatred and separation between North and South after the Civil War. It is love, not vengeance, that will break down the barriers between East and West today, and enable us to realize the peace for which all yearn.

෴

Making Judgments

HE BIBLE IS eternally contemporary because it deals with themes that are basic and relevant in our everyday lives. Some of the words of Scripture puzzle us, and we ponder their meanings. Throughout my ministry, the question asked of me more than any other has been: "How do we interpret the words of Jesus, 'Judge not, that ye be not judged.'?" It is a difficult question to answer.

We cannot believe Jesus meant those words to be taken literally, for he did not take them literally himself. The New Testament is filled with accounts of judgments Jesus made. Jesus knew, as we do, that it is inevitable in this life that human beings will hold opinions and express them. Almost every day of our lives, we are called upon to make judgments on what we see or hear.

I was made aware of this while listening to a sermon on my car radio. The preacher said members of any religion other than Christianity are automatically denied the possibility of salvation in the world to come. Although he is an adult, this man is still in spiritual diapers. I should hate to have anyone think I am unfair or un-Christian when I make such a judgment concerning this man's theology, but it seems to me his conclusion is untenable.

Judgment in this instance—in the determination of the destiny of the soul—is a judgment to be reserved only for God.

However, we must make other judgments each day, in a variety of ways. Every time we read a book, or listen to music, or go to a play or movie, it is natural that we decide whether we like it or not, and we make a judgment about it. If we did not, it would be a sign that we are lacking in intelligence. Perhaps the secret of successful living is simply the ability to make the right judgments.

The critical faculty of human beings is a priceless possession. Criticism has become such an important part of all art that it is a profession in itself. Though we are often in disagreement with music and art critics, their service in helping us sort out the good from the bad is often of real value to us all. Fortunately, or unfortunately, they are prone to sharpen, or soften, their criticism by the way they express it, as was the criticism of one drama critic of a play he had just seen: "There was only one thing wrong with the play: the curtain was up."

When we remember Jesus' words, "Judge not, that ye be not judged..." it is well to keep in mind the words that follow, "...for with what judgment ye judge, ye shall be judged." We reveal ourselves most clearly in the judgments we make of others. Have you ever noticed that it is very seldom a humble person who brings a charge of conceit against another? A complaint against another's selfishness is seldom a sign of our own unselfishness. Those who consider others intolerant are often not tolerant themselves.

Our biting criticisms of others, our mean gossiping and petty slanders, record judgments that are far more telling against ourselves than against those at whom our remarks are leveled. I guess one of the truest tests of independent judgment is being able to admire someone who dislikes us. It is interesting and revealing to note that the harsh judgments Jesus made were never against people, personally. They were always against the principles or ideas that motivated the actions or thoughts of the people involved.

Making judgments, particularly about other people, is often an unconscious attempt to hide our own faults. One of the easiest, but most damaging, ways of building up our own ego is to concentrate on what is wrong with our neighbor. A group of English jurists, meeting to draw up some resolutions for the queen, had begun their statement with the words, "Being conscious as we are of our own defects," when one jurist said, "Gentlemen, we cannot lie to Her Majesty. Change it to 'Being conscious as we are of one another's defects.'"

How easy it is to believe that the words of counsel we hear apply mostly to others. The mature avoid that pitfall. Longfellow once wrote in his diary: "John Ware of Cambridge preached a good sermon. I applied it to myself."

A proverb that has lodged in my mind for a long time is helpful here: "Humor is a handy tool on the critic's workbench." Few have mastered that tool as well as Will Rogers. It was the humor he combined with his most pointed remarks that disarmed the world. There was often stinging criticism in what he had to say, but he dipped his barbs in honey, and they became palatable even to those to whom they were directed.

A victim of his criticism remarked that Will Rogers was like a dentist who pulled your tooth first and then gave you laughing gas. Kind people, like Rogers, have the wisdom and compassion to estimate people not by what they have done, but by what they truly desire to do and be. They do not simply consider the mistakes and the wrongs.

∽

Diverse Opinions

OME TIME AGO, in answer to a reader's request about fundamentalism, and details of my own theology, I gave a brief summary of my religious pilgrimage from conservative beginnings to a broader interpretation of Christian faith.

Both the *Seattle Times* and I received letters, many of them in opposition to my conclusions. As I always try to do, I answered those who wrote to me personally, who signed their letters and gave a return address.

I have always admired people who feel deeply enough about an issue to identify their names with it and share their convictions with others. That those who wrote to me were in disagreement with my conclusions is not the central issue. I have never seen a difference of opinion as an occasion for estrangement. Certainly, vindictiveness is never called for among Christians, for it betrays the all-inclusive, unconditional love we profess.

People know that the one thing we have in common is that we are all different. Lovers of liberty must expect and even urge diversity. When everyone thinks alike, nobody thinks. We seldom learn anything from someone who always agrees with us. Early in my ministry, I read words spoken to the students at Dartmouth College by Ralph Waldo Emerson. Those words became a guide for my ministry—and still are:

"Be content with a little light, so it be your own."

Explore and explore. Be neither chided nor flattered out of your perpetual inquiry. Neither dogmatize or accept another's dogmatism.

The surest antidote to fallacious thinking is correct thinking. The person who has really learned to think has learned the importance of securing certain data and evaluating it. Such people have acquired the power of discriminating between make-believe and fact, between false and intellectually defensible conclusions.

A life of faith is a ceaseless, unremitting quest—a series of rebirths—each leading to a new discovery and a new birth. It is sad if we die before we are fully born. Some things we believe remain forever firm, but at times, the growing process and new discoveries mean giving up what was once a cherished belief.

This releasing—if of a long held idea—is often a painful process. It is no disgrace to alter our opinion. It is not evidence of fickleness, instability, or a lack of faith. It is a mark of humility. We do not receive a dissipation of our faith as we continue our quest. Indeed, it is our faith that eggs us on to new discovery and rebirth. For the deeper we dig, the deeper and firmer becomes the foundation of our faith.

The greatest need of our day is for a combination of open-mindedness that makes way for progress, with the loyalty of convictions that conserve the contributions of the past. We must have a union of clear thinking with devotion to worthy and enduring values.

We people of conservative and liberal temperament must, make up our minds to work together. We need each other. And in our deepest and our best desire to follow Christ, we both want the same thing—vital personal religion of the kind that produces character and sends out unselfish people to build a kingdom of love.

John Wesley once said to some people who were criticizing his methods: "If thy heart is as my heart, here is my hand." There is something of great integrity and common sense in the willingness to work with those with whom we do not always agree.

I would like to emphasize that religion is more than the theologies that define it. Religion is a melding of mind and heart. It is living with the constant consciousness of the continuing presence of God who made us. It is the knowledge that God sustains and guides us whether we ask for it or not, but especially if we ask.

We live in a world whose creatures, though called to community, have practiced the arts of hostility and enmity, to the vast neglect of the arts of love.

It is not ours to cast the stone of judgment, but to offer the helping, healing hand of love and reconciliation. It is not ours to assign blame, but to accept responsibility for ourselves and to act with charity toward others. It is not ours to proceed self-righteously and vindictively, but to walk humbly, penitently, and searchingly toward the truth that will truly set us free.

Nurture Spirit of Love

EHIND SHARP DIFFERENCES of speech, dress, and custom, people everywhere are united in their basic yearning for love and acceptance. The world is one with respect to human needs and feelings. Barriers that separate people must be fashioned into bridges. Enemies must become friends.

This truth was emphasized over and over in the life and teachings of Jesus. Whatever each person's perception of Jesus may be, we cannot dismiss that the Bible reveals Jesus as a teacher without equal. From the beginning of the gospels we read the words, "And he opened his mouth and taught them."

There is a serious omission in our perception of Jesus' teachings when we do not see clearly that he taught that separation from community with others was a tragic thing, perhaps the most tragic that could befall a person. It shines out from throughout the Sermon on the Mount and is made the theme of many of the parables.

Jesus gave top priority to the kingdom of right relationships. "If you bring your gift to the altar, and there remember that your brother has something against you, leave your gift before the altar and go your way. First be reconciled to your brother, and then come and offer your gift." (Matthew 5:23-24)

Jesus' teachings are not just a code of conduct but a call to a community of concern.

But we live in a world whose creatures, though called to community, have practiced the arts of hostility and enmity, to the vast neglect of the arts of love and acceptance of one another.

It is the spirit of love and acceptance of diversity that must be nurtured.

Such a spirit, tolerant, gracious, and charitable, offers a basis for happy and harmonious community life. It is more than a mere amenity. It is more positive than forbearance. It means respect for the beliefs, practices, and habits of others without necessarily sharing or accepting them.

The first line of democratic defense in our nation is not against an external foe but against the internal loss of those ideas and ideals that must in every generation reproduce democracy. If ours is to be a great and loving country, there are high standards that must be met. The strength of our nation is the composite of each individual's integrity. ("No possible rearrangement of bad eggs will ever make a good omelet.")

Dictatorships can, in a way, be inherited. They rest upon coercion. And a tyrant, if he be skillful and powerful enough, can pass on to his successor the regime he has by force established—as has been done in many a dynasty.

But democracy is spiritually engendered in the hearts of its individual citizens. It depends on qualities of personal character, the responsible use of freedom, the willingness to hear and weigh contrary opinions debated in the state, and an inner devotion to the public good that makes outer coercion unnecessary. Depending on these qualities that cannot be coerced, the democratic faith and spirit must be continuously reborn. If the inner qualities that created democracy in the first place are not renewed, its outward forms will fall into decay.

Edwin Markham described the spirit of magnanimity:

> *He drew a circle that shut me out—*
> *Heretic, rebel, a thing to flout.*
> *But love and I had the wit to win:*
> *We drew a circle that took him in.*

Such a man was Booker T. Washington, struggling against deep-seated white prejudice to establish Tuskegee Institute in Alabama. As he passed the mansion of a wealthy woman to whom he was just another black, he heard her call out, "Come here, boy, I need some wood chopped."

Without a word, Washington peeled off his jacket, picked up the ax and went to work, not only cutting and piling the wood, but carrying some into the house.

He had scarcely left when a servant of the household said, "That was Professor Washington, ma'am." Abashed, the woman went to the institute to apologize. The educator replied, "There's no need for an apology, madam. I'm delighted to do favors for my friends."

The woman became one of Tuskegee's warmest and most generous supporters. Washington refused to be disturbed by insult or persecution. "I will permit no man," he said, "to narrow and degrade my soul by making me hate him."

Washington never forgot a kindness and never remembered a wrong. He believed that good character comes by commitment to all that is just, loving, and fair. This begins within each individual. It is always more than a veneer or outward show. It is an inner, heartfelt commitment.

> *There is a destiny that makes us brothers*
> *None goes his way alone*
> *And all that we send into the life of others*
> *Comes back into our own.*

∽

CHERISHING

Joy of Leisure

NE OF THE secrets of a whole and useful life is recognition of the importance of using leisure hours in constructive ways. What we do when we have nothing to do determines a large measure of our usefulness and conditions our spiritual and mental health.

Triviality is perhaps the most characteristic and besetting sin of Americans. Valuable "free" time is frittered away in a succession of activities that lack any serious recreative purpose. Great books remain unread, inspiring music unheard, the marvelous world out of doors goes uncultivated and unappreciated, letters are not written, and friendship calls neglected. Television encourages a sedentary life and the exercise we had intended must wait till tomorrow.

We need a new theology of leisure that sees time as a divine gift and that recognizes that there must be wisdom in choosing what occupies our time beyond working hours.

Unfortunately, in too many instances, the schools still educate largely for work, even though the threat of moral decay is not centered in the hours we spend earning our bread. Education for leisure is too often left entirely to chance.

No one wants continuous leisure or idleness. George Bernard Shaw pointed out that, "A perpetual holiday is a working definition of hell." In a well ordered life, work and leisure blend harmoniously. We pity those who don't know how to work. They do not know the joy of leisure. It is a matter of balance.

Unfortunately, our whole ethical system is based on the virtue of work. Leisure has often been equated with idleness, which in turn is said to breed mischief and sin. "Idle hands," we have been told, "are the devil's workshop." We have accepted the stern dictate of Thomas Carlyle, the philosopher of the Industrial Revolution, that, "Work alone is noble." Nonsense. When work becomes and end in itself, when one cannot enjoy the things for which he has worked because he is too weary or doesn't have the time or desire to enjoy them, work is clearly a liability.

Too often, to our detriment, we carry our work habits over into our leisure hours. Americans do not go bowling when the spirit moves us. We join a bowling league, which means that we are obligated to show up every Monday evening at eight o'clock, as if punching a time clock at a factory. We read not for fun but to improve our minds. We take a walk not to see and smell the flowers, but to keep cholesterol levels down.

Years ago people played all kinds of games. They took them seriously, but they never failed to *play* them. The biblical word for play comes from a root meaning "to laugh." Games are meant to be fun. When games become grim, play becomes work. Rabindranath Tagore, the great Hindu poet, said, "God respects me when I work, but he loves me when I sing and dance."

Work is important, but so is home, friendship, and worship. A busy father hurried home from his office late in the evening with bulging briefcase in hand. He gobbled the evening meal as was his custom and then disappeared into his study. "Mommy," inquired the six-year-old daughter, "why can't Daddy ever spend any time with us after a meal?" "You must remember, honey," explained her mother, "your Daddy is a very busy man. There is always more to do at the office than he can ever get done." "I know, Mommy," she replied, "but why don't they put Daddy into a slower group?" Many times I've stood by the bedside of men who were dying. Never have I heard one say, "I wish I had spent more time at the office."

Every busy person owes it to himself, as well as to his relatives, friends, and associates, to slow up, moderate the pressure, take time out. We must learn to let go, to learn how to hold on. There should be rhythms in life, as there are rhythms in nature: first stress of toil, and then happy release from it; first diligent service, and then rewarding rest or creative activity.

Lee Iacocca's autobiography is a book to which I return from time to time to reread sections that I marked at an earlier hour. It is not by chance that he holds such a high position of leadership. He is wise in the allocation of his time—working hard, but providing in his busy schedule time for rest stops and constructive leisure time activities. He writes:

> Over the years I've had many executives come to me
> and say with pride: "Boy, last year I worked so hard
> that I didn't take any vacation." It's actually nothing
> to be proud of. I always feel like responding: "You
> dummy. You mean to tell me that you can take
> responsibility for an $80 million project and you
> can't plan two weeks out of a year to go off with your
> family and have some fun?" If you want to make good
> use of your time, you've got to know what's most
> important and then you give it all you've got.

W.H. Davies never wrote a poem with more challenge in it for our hurrying, feverish age than when he
composed the lines:

> *What is life, if full of care*
> *We have no time to stand and stare,*
> *No time to stand beneath the boughs*
> *and stare as long as sheep and cows,*
> *No time to see in broad daylight*
> *streams of stars, like skies at night.*
> *A poor life this, if full of care,*
> *We have no time to stand and stare.*

∾

Power of Silence

HE IMPORTANT ISSUES are decided in privacy, behind closed doors, without the blowing of trumpets or waving of banners.

Those great events in our lives that are either joyful or tragic do not make or break us. They merely reveal what we have become in hours of solitude and seclusion. It is in the hours of isolation and withdrawal that we prepare for what life may bring.

The secret thoughts we cherish, the inner companionship of ideas that we harbor, the pictures that we hold in our minds, lie behind that which ultimately becomes action in our lives. A man steals with his mind before he steals with his hands.

Preparation is the key when it comes to succeeding on the playing field, in the classroom, or in life. Before a team runs onto the field, there are hours spent in conditioning through calisthenics, running, and sharpening of skills. What happens in the game reflects this mental and physical preparation.

The untutored eye sees only the performance, but the wise spectator knows that a staggering number of hours and rigorous disciplines are required to achieve excellence.

Long before a student walks into a classroom for an examination he earns the *A, B,* or *C.* In silence some secluded nook or cubicle of a library, the pupil battles to master the subject and earn the grade.

The point is clear: to hope and even pray for success and neglect the laws of learning is to make a mockery of the laws by which we learn. It is not enough to want to master a subject. One must pay the price. Dirt is cheap, but one must dig for gold. The island of excellence is surrounded by a sea of sweat.

The teacher who lectures knows that he must study over the material privately before he presents it publicly if he is to be exciting and helpful.

The same type of private preparation is necessary for the preaching ministry. What goes on in the pastor's study reflects what goes on in the pulpit and ultimately in the congregation. Private evasions become public liabilities and the preacher's laziness is shouted from the housetops.

Regardless of his talent, popularity, experience, reputation, and past successes, a wise preacher builds each sermon on the rock of preparation and not on the sands of over-confidence and carelessness. There is nothing sadder than an empty preacher pouring himself out to a full house.

Without a den of refuge, no tranquillity or greatness can be achieved. Thomas Jefferson wrote the Declaration of Independence in a quiet rooming house in Philadelphia. The soaring ideas that went into it evolved during hours of reading and contemplation in a secluded library. Had it been a TV or guest room, the United States might still be a colony. Nothing is accomplished in a crowd. We grow when we are alone.

Noah built the ark before the waters came. It was in the silence of the Tekoan Hills that Amos became a prophet of the invisible realities. In the loneliness of the long night watches, David became a poet and Moses a seer.

The battle for high ideals and worthy actions is not won mainly in the hour of temptation but in hours of silence and isolation when we nurture our highest aspirations.

Sabbath

HE TEN COMMANDMENTS represent the great ethical principles upon which the foundation of civilization is laid. Each commandment is important, but in this day and age when more activities are packed into fewer hours—more to do than we can ever get done—it is well for us to heed the wise counsel of the Fourth Commandment: Remember the Sabbath day to keep it holy.

The idea of one day each week when there would be a cessation from everything that could be called work was not a Hebrew innovation. The observance of one day for rest was also present in Assyrian and Babylonian cultures. The commandment at first was merely to rest from work, but as time went by, it evolved into a complicated system of restrictions—of dos and don'ts. In the time of Jesus there were thirty-nine types of work prohibited on the Sabbath, subdivided into 1,521 prohibitions.

Many were trivial regulations. To dig in a garden on the Sabbath, as some do today, was punishable by death. The ox that fell into a ditch on the Sabbath stayed there.

No fire was to be kindled on the Sabbath. If death threatened, a physician could be called, but a fracture could not be set.

A woman was forbidden to look into a mirror on the Sabbath, lest seeing a gray hair she be tempted to pluck it—that would be reaping! A generation before the birth of Jesus, two great Jewish schools of thought led by Shammai and Hillel discussed, debated, and disagreed on an earth-shaking subject: Could an egg laid on the Sabbath be eaten? Obviously, the hen was laboring on this day prescribed for rest.

These laws, instead of being a blessing to the Jews, as they ought to have been, became a grievous burden to be borne or evaded by trickery. No wonder Jesus rejected so many of these regulations, telling the Pharisees that they were straining at gnats and swallowing camels, and neglecting the weightier matters of the law. They were keeping rituals but neglecting the things of the spirit—love, justice, and mercy.

There are many today who disregard the Sabbath or Sunday because of unfavorable impressions of the day gathered in their youth. Some remember some mighty drab Sundays spent with their families, relatives, or friends, who observed the Sabbath day with very strict regulations.

Ruskin once said that Monday morning was the happiest morning of the week because it would be six days until Sunday rolled around again. No wonder the old idea of heaven being a place where Sabbaths never end didn't appeal to many people.

It is too bad that many, in throwing out the husks,

throw out the fruit as well. A day of rest fulfills a law of life. Rest is one of the imperatives of creation. The earth, spinning on its axis, has periods of light and dark. The farmer knows that land is more productive when there is a rotation of crops, or a period when the field lies fallow.

What nature imposes by law, humans are supposed to know by reason. We need one day each week for rest and relaxation—one full day when the pressure is off. The bow that is always bent loses its strength. "I can do a year's work in eleven months," Henry Ward Beecher once said, "but not in twelve." He might have added that he could do a week's work in six days, but not in seven.

The demand for rest for those who labor physically is obvious. Fatigue demands repose and restoration. But those who work mainly with their minds are likely to be caught in a whirl when they think business and duties are so important they cannot take a day off. In the brain are areas where certain functions, such as seeing and hearing, are localized. When one area functions for a long time, to the exclusion of others, depression and fatigue set in.

Jesus understood the necessity of alternating activity and repose. After a busy day, he said, "Let us go apart into a desert place and rest awhile." He knew there must be alternation from movement to meditation, from society to solitude, from companionship with people to companionship with God.

He knew that in his life, there must be a time for receptivity—for a wise passiveness when God's wisdom and love could flow into his life with healing power.

In Europe, in days gone by, there were wayside shrines where a traveler could pause for rest, reflection, and meditation. Once in a while, we see such shrines in America, but they are few and far between. In the procession of days, however, Sunday comes calling us to rest. Worship becomes not a refuge from work, but a source of renewal.

Too many of us are all sail and no anchor. "Twice in every twenty-four hours," wrote Gaius Glen Atkins, one of America's great clerics, "the tides of the ocean, soiled and discolored through their contact with our shores, withdraw themselves into the bosom of the deep, there to be cleansed in the clean salt immensity of the sea..."

Life is like that. We, too, are much stained through our contact with occupation or pleasure. We need to let the tides of God's love move into our lives so that we may go forth better able to cope with life's problems.

> *O sabbath rest by Galilee!*
> *O calm of hills above!*
> *Where Jesus knelt to share with thee*
> *The silence of eternity*
> *Interpreted by love.*

> *Drop thy still dews of quietness*
> *Till all our strivings cease.*
> *Take from our souls the strain and stress*
> *And let our ordered lives confess*
> *The beauty of thy peace.*

Hours Apart

HEN I WAS a young man I worshiped in a church where we sang the same hymn at least once a month: "Work, For the Night Is Coming." One line of the hymn encouraged us to "work while the dew is sparkling." So we did. It was good counsel then and good counsel now.

We all have just so much time. We cannot create more hours than the twenty-four God gives us. But in a very true sense we can capitalize on certain periods of the day and compress a vast amount of work into a short period.

I am referring to the early morning hours. The term is a loose one, meaning 5:00 a.m. to some and 8:00 a.m. to others. Then, if ever, come perfect moments of uninterrupted concentration for good, solid work or for reading, writing, meditating, for devotions, Bible study, and prayer.

Many great spiritual leaders have found and used the morning hours while others slept. Muriel Lester, a great British mystic, set her alarm for two each morning. In the stillness of the morning she was attuned to the small voice of her Creator. John Wesley arose at five o' clock or earlier, prayed, read the Bible, and was on his horse by six.

"And Jesus, arising a great while before dawn, departed into a solitary place and there he prayed." Not without reason have the monastic orders of the ages required early-morning devotions.

Many Americans remember Kirby Page for his prolific social-action teachings and writings. But that was only one side of the man, as his many writings on the spiritual life reveal. When and how did he find the time to dig so deep? A friend of mine discovered the answer when he was a young man working at the Silver Bay, New York, conference grounds where Dr. Page was the chief resource leader at a large conference. Part of my friend's job was to sweep the front porch of the conference hotel at five o'clock every morning.

Each morning as he began sweeping he saw a man come out of the hotel, carrying a Bible and another book or two. The man would greet him with a quiet hello and walk to a point on beautiful Lake George far away from the hotel. Here he would stay until 6:30 and then return to his room before most of those he ministered to had even thought of getting up. Thus did Kirby Page replenish his mind and spirit.

Even so, some people work best at night. Dr. Ralph Sockman, the great Methodist minister, thought he often did his best work from midnight to 2:00 a.m. Despite his time setting, Sockman's best working period has the same essential as that of the early morning: a designated time apart from the many interruptions of

the hurly-burly of midday,

If a generalization may be made, it might be this: What people do with these hours apart determines what life will do to them.

Fat accumulates first, despite all visible evidence to the contrary, not around the waistline, but inside the cranium. Those who would have spiritual power must daily be refreshed. There can be no devotion without devotions—devotions gleaned not from a self-help book planned by some New York publisher, but from deep sources and disciplined attention to important concerns.

If we are to pray for some friend in need, we must have time to pray. If the Bible is to speak to us and through us to others, then it must not be forced to compete with the insignificant busy-ness which eats up the hours.

If the difficult process called "study" is to be fruitful, some uninterrupted span of hours must be found.

Gone So Fast

N A SUNDIAL in an old english garden are inscribed these words: "It is later than you think."

All of us in some way or other have had this truth impressed upon us. It may have been through an unusually revealing glimpse of ourselves in the mirror or by means of the aging appearance of some of our contemporaries. Perhaps it came from a sudden realization that those of a younger generation had reached maturity and were stepping into positions of leadership.

When it dawns on us that it is "later than we think," we remember some of the things that we had once confidently hoped to do but still have not done. Then we realize, as we have never before, the preciousness of time.

We remember some of the old copybook maxims like the aphorism of Horace Mann: "Lost somewhere between sunrise and sunset two golden hours, set with sixty diamond minutes. No reward is offered for they are lost forever."

Or possibly more of us will recall Benjamin

Franklin's, "Dost thou love life? Then do not squander time, for that is the stuff life is made of."

Sometimes we are prone to regard the epigrammatic wisdom of other generations as but the expression of the essence of the commonplace. This may be true. It behooves us, however, to keep in mind that much of the prudential wisdom of our fathers is not to be dismissed with a few supercilious shrugs.

Many people of superlative endowments have failed to measure up to their possibilities for the simple reason that they have never learned to use the moments that are theirs. None of us would think of throwing away the nickels, dimes, and quarters that accumulate in our pockets. But almost all of us do throw away the small change of time—five minutes here, a quarter hour there—that accumulates in an ordinary day.

Unfortunately, large blocks of time are often frittered away in trivial pursuits. Dr. Albert Fitch, the great American clergyman and educator, tells of walking through one of the dormitories of an ancient educational institution. The door of one of the rooms was open. It revealed an atmosphere blue with smoke and a group of disheveled youths lounging around a table playing cards for a trivial stake. Two hours later Dr. Fitch passed through the same building and noticed the same group still engaged in their all-consuming occupation.

Dr. Fitch was not opposed to games and recreation, and he knew the importance of relaxation, yet he thought of the wealth of privilege all around that these young men were missing: gymnasiums for the body, a library greater than that of ancient Alexandria, men and

"He learned the value of 5 minutes"

youth seeking the noble and gracious things of life, outside the glory of a bracing winter day.

On the other hand, here sat this band of privileged young people abusing their freedom and leisure by imitating grooms of the stable matching coins in the harness room. What a picture. And how often it can be duplicated!

Herbert Spencer, the English philosopher, enjoyed an occasional game of billiards. When he was beaten at the game he enjoyed quoting the remark of another member of the Athenaeum Club, that excessive skill at this game was evidence of a misspent youth.

This somewhat ill-natured comment is by no means without truth. The habitual winner of bridge prizes may well have sacrificed some of the higher concerns in becoming adept at shuffling cards. John Ruskin was right: "If you do this you cannot do that."

One of the most banal phrases in the English language is the expression "killing time." The individual who has to seek some way of putting in the hours is an example of human maladjustment.

Browning has Rabbi Ben Ezra say, "How good to live and learn." He who finds it a problem to dispose of his time is not living; he is merely vegetating. All around us are fields of intellectual activity which challenge every scintilla of mentality which we possess.

We cannot take all knowledge to be our province. To keep ourselves moderately informed in regard to a few of the ever-widening fields of thought taxes our capacity to the utmost.

This, however, is not all of life. On every side of us

are good causes which are languishing because of lack of leadership or loyal followers, In such a world the wasting of time is not simply a harmless peccadillo.

Henry David Thoreau tells us that we cannot kill time without injuring eternity. Time is the arbiter of destiny. It is the material of which our lives are built.

The psalmist offered a prayer that is relevant in every generation: "Teach us how short our life is, so that we may become wise." (Psalm 90:12)

L O V I N G

Courtesy

HE ANCIENT ROMANS believed that May was a bad luck month. Many couples planning their wedding ceremonies leapfrogged May and set the date for their vows in June. June became known as the wedding month.

But while June remains a popular month for weddings, it is rivaled by the fall and Christmas seasons.

Happily, love is a flower that blossoms and grows without the aid of seasons. The time when vows are made is not as important as the quality of character carried into the union.

One of the most interesting personalities ever to appear on the American scene was H.L. Mencken, an editor, writer, and satirist. He was a brilliant individualist, with a flair for using words. He had opinions on everything, and since most of his statements had humorous overtones, he was extremely popular with reporters.

Mencken did not marry until he was in his middle years, but when he finally did announce his plans, it was a tremendously newsworthy event.

One of many questions asked by the battery of

reporters surrounding him was, "What is the most important ingredient in a successful marriage?" Without the slightest hesitation, Mencken replied, "Courtesy."

The reporters, expecting him to say something funny, were already wearing broad smiles when they realized there was nothing funny in what Mencken had said. They also realized that he had managed to put into one word what marriage experts usually took three hundred pages and a hundred thousand words to say.

It was obvious that Mencken had given marriage a lot of thought, and if there is one word in our language that will keep a marriage going through the years, that word would have to be *courtesy*. Courtesy is more easily understood than love because it is more specific.

In the well-known "love" chapter of First Corinthians, Saint Paul gives us the definition of what love is and is not. As great as this chapter is, people still find loopholes in it. Take kindness, for instance. What is kind for one person or in one situation may not be kind for another person or another situation. However, courtesy is easily recognized.

One of my friends, an attorney, is renowned for his competence and fairness. I admire him for his legal skills, but it is his thoughtfulness and courtesy to others that I will always most remember. His courtesies are everywhere in evidence, but his family members love him most because his courtesies are at their height within the home. He is faithful to his larger responsibilities as husband and father and is not neglectful of the amenities.

He calls if he knows he will be delayed for dinner.

Each family member, regardless of age, is treated as a person whose opinion deserves to be heard. He never enters the room of even the youngest without knocking. He is considerate of the needs of others at the meal table. He does not claim the bathroom as his own.

Several times when he was not aware of my seeing, I noticed him opening the car door for his wife. He makes untrue four lines that have lodged in my mind for years:

> *I don't know much of decorum and such,*
> *But this one thing I know to be true.*
> *When a man helps his wife getting into the car,*
> *One or the other is new.*

When I was a young man working as the director of recreation at a YMCA camp in Ohio, I had opportunity to listen to many visiting speakers. One speaker, eager to guide the steps of the nearly three hundred boys who were present, left with each camper a copy of a poem entitled, "A Gentleman." I still have my copy, and think of my attorney friend each time I recall it:

> *He thinks of you before himself*
> *He serves you if he can*
> *For in whatever company*
> *The manners make the man.*
> *At ten or forty, 'tis the same*
> *The manners tell the tale*
> *And I discern the gentleman*
> *By signs that never fail.*

I do not know whether similar lines have been written for women. But if they have not, they should be, because courtesy is for everybody.

～

The Gentle Art

OT ALL WHO hear have learned to listen. There
is a difference between listening and hearing.
Listening is a conscious effort to hear and to
understand what is being heard. The act of listening requires more than simply letting sound waves
into our ears, just as reading requires more than looking at the print. Listening demands active participation.
It requires effort. Listening is an acquired art. We learn
to speak in two years, but we spend a lifetime trying to
learn how to listen. Perhaps the fact that we have two
ears and only one tongue is a symbol that we are
intended to listen twice as much as we speak.

Many good things can happen when we develop the
gift of listening—listening with attention, listening with
awareness, listening with discernment, listening with
creativity, and listening with empathy,

Listening is the first duty of love. There is a way of
listening that surpasses all compliments. When we give
our undivided attention to another we affirm that individual. We say, "You are important. I want to hear what
you have to say." It is human nature to desire to be

heard. George Bernard Shaw said, "My idea of a good conversation is to find someone who will listen to me."

Dr. Karl Menninger, who died in 1990, was a gifted doctor and writer, an inspiring speaker, and a great listener. Among his many memorable comments was his statement that the central purpose of each life is to dilute the misery of the world. He believed that one of the ways we do this is by listening with love and empathy to everyone with whom we visit. In his book, *Love Against Hate*, he wrote, "Listening is a magnetic and strange thing—a creative force. The friends who listen to us are the ones we move toward, and we want to sit in their radius. When we are listened to, it creates us, makes us unfold and expand. I discovered this a few years ago. Before that, when I went to a party I would think anxiously: 'Now try hard. Be lively.' But now I tell myself to listen with affection to anyone who talks to me.

It is reassuring to know that usefulness in life is not confined to the brilliant, wealthy, articulate, or physically attractive individuals. God can use even the least of us, provided we learn to listen.

> *His thoughts were slow*
> *His words were few*
> *and never formed to glisten*
> *But he was a joy to all his friends,*
> *You ought to have seen him listen.*

Many positives come when we learn to listen. Calvin Coolidge said, "No one ever listened himself out of a job." Yogi Bera remarked, "It is amazing what you can see when you listen." His phraseology is always creatively startling, but his point is clear.

If we listen, we open the door to the possibility of learning something new. When we speak, we hear only what we already know. Knowledge has never been known to enter the head via an open mouth. The wise and humble can sometimes receive information by listening to others on crucial issues. It happened on separate occasions to both Thomas "Tip" O'Neill, former speaker of the House, and to Governor Buddy Roemer of Louisiana.

O'Neill went to Boston College in 1967 to argue for the merits of American involvement in Vietnam. His son Tommy and daughter Susan were students at the college. The audience gave him a rough time in the question period. O'Neill claimed that he had been briefed at the highest levels and did some shameless name dropping. Then a student got up and asked, "Have you ever been briefed by the other side?" O'Neill brooded about that remark. He began to listen to ideas other than those he had held previously, and his views changed totally.

When Roemer was pondering whether to sign the nation's strictest abortion bill, he listened to his estranged wife, Patti, his twenty-three-year-old daughter Caroline and three women members of his Cabinet. "All" Roemer said, "independently arrived at the same conclusion: veto."

Heeding their counsel, Roemer vetoed the bill. He made clear in a subsequent speech that his once firm and unqualified opposition to abortion evolved into a broader concept because he had listened to what the women had to say.

In Luke 2:46 we read: "And they found Jesus in the Temple, sitting among the teachers, listening to them and asking them questions." Note the order. The young Jesus was listening before he asked questions. He was face to face with the great Hebrew tradition, which had been accumulating for more than fifteen hundred years. He did not rush in with "What is the sense of this?" or "Why do you do that?" He listened. He heard what they had to say. He knew the wisdom of listening in order to ask intelligent questions.

Unfortunately, some omit the listening process today, and, in the words of G.K. Chesterton, "They know the last word about everything and the first word about nothing." Because they have not listened themselves into knowledge, they become part of the problem and not part of the answer.

Above all, Jesus encouraged his followers to listen, as did Elijah, for the still small voice of God. Humans, are inclined to hammer away at God, telling their own plans and wishes and often reserving little or no time to listen for and understand the plan of the Supreme Architect. God does not speak in an audible voice, but sensitive souls, by listening in silence, can learn to perceive the Creator's will.

It is wise to pray simply: "O God, of whom we ask so much, help us to listen to what thou dost ask of us."

Different Seasons

CTOBER GAVE A *party*
The leaves by hundreds came
The ashes and the maples
And those of every name.

—George Cooper, 1838-1937

Each season has its own, peculiar delights. I love all seasons of the year. I love winter. I love clear, cold nights. I love to see the stars like silver nails driven into the black vault of heaven. I love the crisp crunch of snow beneath my feet, the frost on window panes, and the warm glow of a log fire.

In the wintertime the earth dies and lies motionless, silent, cold, and stiff. When the crocus pokes its head through frosted soil, it brings intimations of the season that is to be. Then comes spring, the angel of resurrection. When spring blows her trumpet, the earth rises on its feet and sings.

I can recall that as a boy I loved wintertime, but I was always hopeful that the season would not go into extra innings and that spring would soon arrive.

Sometimes spring came with snowflakes in her hair, but they were just for the moment, and the world soon became a palace of beauty, fashioned without the sound of a hammer.

There was delicacy of tint, subtlety of shadow—a loveliness beyond description. The greening grass, flowering shrub, and blossoming bush delighted the eye and provided indescribable fragrance to all the world around.

I love winter. I love spring, but I love summer, too. I love the gentle litany of the winds in the tops of the trees. I love the long evenings and the song of the birds. "What is so rare as a day in June? Then, if ever, come perfect days; then heaven tries earth if it be in tune, and over it softly her warm ear lays."

I love the coast in summertime—every beach swept twice each day by the great broom of the sea, and the therapy of water calming even the most restless of nerves.

I love winter. I love spring. I love summer, but it is fall that I love most of all. Autumn combines the best of summer's mellow sunshine which, like a blessing, is warm and golden, plus the cool nights of spring. To this she adds a breathtaking profusion of color. The woodlands, virtually ablaze, are like bonfires set to welcome winter.

Roadways become crowded with people viewing the outdoor show. Some are doubly rewarded by a glimpse here and there of an "old-time" cornfield, with pumpkins squatting around their cornstalk wigwams under such beautiful skies that even the breezes whistle at it.

Many of our birds, having perfected their Southern accents, are gone, and we note dead leaves whispering together, then tiptoeing up the walks and scratching at our doors.

There are two views of autumn, as there are of life itself. Poets like to write of autumn's glories; others just think of her as an untidy housekeeper throwing things away. She uses what seems to many a vast, windy broom, torrents of water, thick suds of snow, and ice, causing the dead boughs to snap and fall. Once-glowing leaves now clog gutters or roots and choke our brooks and ponds. What is not gathered for trash heaps will quietly rot and enrich the soil where it lies. In this process we, too, can learn a valuable lesson.

There are many things we need to shed—prejudices, dusty intolerances, bad hits and errors of all kinds that have clung too long. We must let them fall like dead leaves to nourish a new growth of love and kindness.

How beautifully, too, the poetry of the fall season renews the soul and lifts the spirit. Edna St. Vincent Millay's lovely poem, "God's World," surfaces to conscious memory:

O world, I cannot hold thee close enough!
Thy winds, thy wide gray skies!
Thy mists that roll and rise!
Thy woods, this autumn day that ache and sag
And all but cry with colour! That gaunt crag
To crush! To lift the lean of that black bluff!
World, World, I cannot get thee close enough!
Long have I known a glory in it all,

But never knew I this;
Here such passion is.
As stretcheth me apart. Lord I do fear
Thou'st made the world too beautiful this year,
My soul is all but out of me—let fall
No burning leaf; prithee let no bird call.

∾

Belief Not Enough

 NE OF GOD'S great gifts—perhaps the greatest gift to each of us—is being born into an unfinished world and given a share with God in creation. We become worthy of this great trust when we commit our lives to the Creator's way of unconditional, non-manipulative, all-accepting love.

It is not enough simply to believe in God. It is commitment to the Creator's will that gives integrity to our faith. Religion is behavior and not mere belief.

The Biblical view of humanity is not one of despair. It affirms that we are made in God's image. We have divine origin, supreme worth, and eternal destiny. No matter how deprived or dissipated humans may sometimes be, they are still God's children loved and accepted. Saint Augustine said, "Dig deep enough into any human being and you will find something divine."

The divinity that resides within all of us may not always be easily discernible. It may be embryonic and undeveloped, but it is, nevertheless, there. We are called to help the weak and distressed realize their highest possibilities.

I like to repeat the story that Adlai Stevenson used to tell of a parishioner who was so deeply moved upon hearing his preacher tell of the needs of the poor and the hungry that he jumped to his feet, crying, "Use me, Lord, use me—in an advisory capacity." I like to repeat that story because there seems to be a ready supply of that kind of dedication.

God does not need more advisers. God needs those who will give practical and effective support by their prayers and service to others—even to their enemies.

In one of his books, author Walter D. Calvert tells the story of Peter Miller, pastor of a small Baptist church in Ephrata, Pennsylvania, during the American Revolution. Miller was much loved by the folks of Ephrata, except by one who scorned all religion and opposed the church on every issue.

No friend of the Colonial cause, this man had been arrested for treason and sentenced to die.

"The minister walked sixty miles," wrote Calvert, "to plead with George Washington for the man's pardon. Regretfully the general shook his head, saying, 'I'm sorry, but I cannot grant your request to spare your friend.' Quietly, Miller replied, 'My friend? He is my worst enemy.' Amazed, Washington exclaimed, 'What! You have walked all this distance to save an enemy? Then how can I do other than pardon him?'"

Without hope for praise or fear of blame, Dr. Martin Luther King Jr. identified himself with the cause of racial justice and equality. In his book, *Stride Toward Freedom*, he wrote:

It has been my conviction ever since reading Walter Rauschenbusch that any religion which professes to be concerned about the souls of men and is not concerned about the social and economic conditions that scar the soul is a spiritually moribund religion only waiting for the day to be buried. It well has been said, "A religion that ends with the individual, ends."

Comedian Dick Gregory talks about an incident from his boyhood that still burns brightly in his memory. He had had a good day selling papers and shining shoes, and he went into a restaurant and got a veritable feast—a bowl of chili, a cheeseburger, a soft drink, and a piece of chocolate cake. As he ate, an old wino came in, ordered twenty-six cents worth of food, and made the most of every bite.

When it came time to pay, the man said simply that he didn't have any money, whereupon the owner knocked him down with a bottle, watched him bleed a little, and then began to kick him.

Young Gregory then said, "Leave him alone. I'll pay the twenty-six cents." But the wino said, "Keep your twenty-six cents. You don't have to pay now. I just finished paying for it." He started to leave, then he put his hand on the boy's shoulder, and with the venom in his voice replaced by sadness, said, "Thanks, sonny, but it's too late now. Why didn't you pay it before?"

Young Gregory realized that he had waited too long to help. He had avoided getting involved, had shrugged something off as not his responsibility. He had done the same thing thirty-eight people had done several years ago in New York City while a girl was being manhandled and murdered. He had done the same thing minor bureaucrats in Hitler's Germany had done.

All believed themselves to be innocent bystanders in an hour of another's need. There are no "innocent" bystanders—certainly not among religious people—for in loving we feel responsible to help others in their time of privation, sorrow, and hunger.

There are millions of people today at the counter of life, hungry, but with no money to pay and no food within reach. There are millions who need others to help them move toward some form of "equality." Those of us who can help cannot do it all, but we can do something.

> *If there be some weaker one, Give me strength*
>   *to help him on;*
> *If a blinder soul there be, Let me guide him*
>   *nearer Thee.*
> *Make my mortal dreams come true*
> *With the work I fain would do;*
> *Clothe with life the weak intent,*
> *Let me be the thing I meant...*

> —John Greenleaf Whittier

Index

Acknowledgments

WITHOUT THE HELP of many generous and supportive
people, this book, not to mention the past sixteen years
of *Seattle Times* columns from which it came, would not
have been possible. I would like to thank everyone who
has played a part in making it a reality. Most especially I
want to thank my wife, Leone, who has supported me in
spirit for fifty years, as well as helping me to get these
words on paper. Alex MacLeod, managing editor of the
Seattle Times and my first editor, has been indispensible
as a friend and advisor, as has everyone at the *Times*.

I would also like to thank Alex Lubertozzi, my editor at High Tide Press, and Ruth Williamson-Kirkland,
whose generous assistance and devotion have been an
inspiration.

About the Author

THE REVEREND DOCTOR Dale Emerson Turner began his official ministry in Lansing, Michigan, in 1943 after graduating from Yale Divinity School. He had intended to become an athletic coach before his graduation from West Virginia Wesleyan College in 1940, and was able to combine this joy with that of youth minister in Lansing and Grand Rapids, Michigan.

In 1948 he accepted a call to become senior minister of Plymouth Congregational Church in Lawrence, Kansas. He served his community's spiritual needs for ten years as pastor, professor of religion at the University of Kansas, and chaplain of the Kansas football team. He was named "Man of the Year" in Lawrence in 1951.

He took the helm at University Congregational Church in Seattle, Washington, in 1958. The compassionate and spirited length of his pastoral shadow cast far and wide throughout the University of Washington community, touching all parts of Seattle and beyond—from ministry in the slums of Japan to the pulpit of Saint Giles Cathedral in Scotland. Since his retirement from the Seattle church in 1982, he has written a weekly column for the Religion page of the *Seattle Times*.

Although Dr. Turner has received many honors, including the Outstanding Alumni Award of West Virginia Wesleyan, the Salvation Army "Others Award," Seattle's "First Citizen" award, the degree of doctor humanis causa from Seattle University, and the endowment of the Dale E. Turner Scholarship Fund at Yale Divinity School, he continues to believe himself to be no particular hero. Instead, he honors and nurtures the bravery in each person he meets and in every individual with whom he is acquainted.

Reverend Turner makes his home in Seattle with his multi-talented wife of fifty years, Leone. They have four sons, three daughters-in-law, six grandsons, and two granddaughters.

A Note on the Type

The text of this book was set in Baskerville, a typeface originally designed by John Baskerville, a printer from Birmingham, England, in 1752. This version, New Baskerville, was created by George Jones for Linotype-Hell in 1930. Baskerville is sturdy yet graceful, displaying long, elegant serifs along with thick vertical strokes. The text of this book was set electronically.

Printed and bound by RR Donnelley & Sons Co.
Crawfordsville, Indiana

Designed by Alex Lubertozzi